BODHENA'S ADVENTURES IN SAMSARA

BODHENA'S ADVENTURES IN SAMSARA

A SANNYASIN MEMOIR

BY SWAMI DEVA BODHENA

OSHO WORLD FOUNDATION

NIYOGI BOOKS

Published by
NIYOGI BOOKS
D-78, Okhla Industrial Area, Phase-I
New Delhi-110 020, INDIA
Tel: 91-11-26816301, 49327000
Fax: 91-11-26810483, 26813830
email: niyogibooks@gmail.com
website: www.niyogibooksindia.com

In association with
Osho World Foundation

C-5/44, Safdarjung Development Area
New Delhi -110016

Cover Design and Layout by Osho World Foundation

ISBN: 978-93-85285-35-6

Publication: 2016

Printed at: Niyogi Offset Pvt. Ltd., New Delhi, India

CONTENTS

Prologue

It has been an interesting experience writing this story, more than ten years ago. Please let me tell you briefly how this happened.

Between late 1977 and early 1989, for most of the time, I used to live in an absolutely extraordinary environment, in the communes around the enlightened mystic Osho. While I had always been aware of the significance of this, it was not until years later, around 2000, that I came more frequently into contact with seekers who were quite curious about that time, and who wanted to know, "Hey, what was it like to be around Osho? How did you live? What did you guys do?" And I was the man who had the goodies ... well, at least a few of them. But how to relate all this over a cup of coffee or two? Almost impossible. However, the question had been put to me, and, as it seems now, a seed had been planted.

In the spring of 2002 I started noticing that there were all kinds of Poona- and Ranch-stories popping up in my head, just welling up, all nicely structured and plotted and formulated. And they kept coming and coming, and at times it felt like it was almost driving me nuts. It has never been my intention to write a 'book', but in March I started to write, if only just to unburden myself. And it was all quite easy, as if the whole thing had been waiting there in my belly to be written down, and it came out in one piece, pretty much in the same form as it is now. Around late summer I lost steam. So I left it there, the way it was, except for corrections and some minor additions and changes. I am still a bit baffled today, jeez, did I really write that? Where did that come from? How did I remember all that stuff? I mean, I had no notes from back then, except for a few from my aborted PhD thesis.

But what to do with it? To step out with it in front of the whole sangha – not me! And ambition has never been one of my stronger character traits. Obviously I needed a bit of help if anything was going to happen with it, and I began sending out some e-copies. I am very grateful for the friends that happened along, read the draft and gave me some encouraging feedback. And after all, it is one of my great pleasures to share Osho, and it appears that is a way for me to do it.

This story is not about 'new revelations', nor was I in a privileged position that would enable me to come up with previously untold hot gossip, about Osho, or the crème de la crème of the commune. I was, and still am, just a 'regular guy', and the story is told from that perspective. Still, each detail, written or unwritten, has its own significance, and in some way has brought me to where I am here and now. It has been a wonderful ride, a challenging encounter with myself, up to this very day.

Peace,

Deva Bodhena
Dehra Dun, India
October 2012

"What a long, strange trip it's been."
- The Grateful Dead, "Truckin"

PART I:
BEFORE

-1-

I started out as a rather straight kid, growing up in a middle-class environment in a small town in the Harz Mountains of northern Germany. Now, many years later, I find myself living in the same place again, but I have changed in a way that I never imagined possible. I seem to have come full circle, in a sense. Yet, when I encounter the people around me, I see myself quite a bit at odds with them. They mirror very much the aspirations and value systems that I had been conditioned with, and I can't say that I feel very much at home in that world any more. I have often scratched my head and wondered, "How the fuck did I get here? What's been happening?" Nowadays I see my first priority in life that of being a spiritual seeker, and I guess most people would think I've gone nuts if I told them how I perceive reality, really. Sure, where they're coming from, they're right. Not much of a problem.

If I look back now, I can see that the seeds had always been there, but they needed time and a suitable environment to start to open and grow. And by no means do I have the impression that the journey is finished now. On the contrary. Outwardly, it may not appear as dramatic any more, but I know that certain processes have been started that have gained their own momentum.

These days, I have pretty much retreated into my own bubble and I feel quite at peace with myself and "the world". I still believe that the socio-economic system that is being practised nowadays is a rather screwed-up way of dealing with reality, but looking at it from the perspective of the Dharma has enabled me to come to terms with it. It is a system rooted in a profound ignorance, and out of this all that suffering is created that we can see around us. For me, that leaves really only one way out, which is *in*. I don't see much of a need to go about messing around with any of the symptoms; I'll leave that to the experts like Mother Theresa and other do-gooders. Let the dead bury the dead.

If anything, this tells me that I have integrated some of my lessons to the point where I can be out here and hold my own, without falling flat on my back. I know I will have to face some issues that I feel lurking underneath the surface, but that will happen when the time is right for it. Nothing to worry about.

So here and now I'll sit down and try to recollect and reflect on some of the stations along the way. And yes, I know ... someday the river is going to take me home.

***

-2-

Looking back, my childhood seems to have been quite uneventful. There are a few things that stick out, though. I have always loved nature, and as a kid I was an avid boy scout, crawling around in the woods, going on hikes and camping trips. In time, my interest shifted and I gradually became more interested in going to our local "Beatkeller" to listen to live rock groups. I loved rock music, the rebelliousness and aliveness of it, and as far as I can recall I was the first Beatles fan in town.

I also loved to read, preferably adventuresome stories about far away places. So when the first opportunity presented itself to go to one, I took it without thinking twice, and with 17 went to America for a year as an exchange student. I stayed with a very nice family in a small town in Michigan, went to high school and took to life there like a duck takes to water. By the time I returned my conditioning had undergone a significant workover, and it took me a few years to balance out some of the effects.

It wasn't until I left my home town and moved to Giessen to attend university that I finally got rolling. The sixties might have been over by then, but the seventies that were wild enough themselves had started, and I just couldn't ignore the pervading zeitgeist. There was something in me that began to question what I saw happening around me. The first layer that I hit was the socio-economic one, and the result was that I experienced a considerable drift to the left. Yet, as much as my new insights appeared to be true to me, I didn't get too much involved in the leftish scene. To me, the guys that frequented certain pubs and hung out there until late at night over many a beer, discussing revolutionary strategies with the smoke of self-rolled cigarettes hanging in the air, seemed to be lacking something.

So I continued to question, and more and more became interested in spiritual topics. To look for answers within the framework of the established Christian religions was out of the question for me. I had been raised as a protestant, but already several years before had quit my membership in the church (very much to the dismay of my parents). I read a few books on eastern mysticism, became a vegetarian, started to do yoga asanas on a regular basis, and eventually got initiated into Transcendental Meditation (TM), which I practised for about a year. However, none of the New Age groups that I came into contact with attracted me very much, neither the Ananda Marga, nor the Hare Krishna, and to me there was something not quite right about that perpetual smile that the TM people were wearing (although the Maharishi seemed to be a nice enough guy - at least he had long hair). And as far as the Jesus Freaks were concerned, well, just forget it.

More than anything else it was traveling that gave my life a sense of purpose in those years. In 1970, I went on a four week trip through France and Spain. Hitchhiking most of the way, I eventually made it across the Strait of Gibraltar to Tangier, where I stayed for a week, my first taste of the Orient (and I also for the first time felt the wrath of Montezuma's Revenge).

In 1971, now at university, I had my first long summer vacation. During those years, as I had learned, the overland route to India was open, and it had increasingly become an in-thing to go there, so I decided to give it a try. I wasn't so much focused on India, I rather wanted to see how far I would get, and what was out there. By chance I had met an Iranian student who wanted to go home for the summer and who was looking for somebody to share the ride in his Volksporsche, a cute, two-seated sports car. That got me as far as Teheran, and the fun was only beginning. I continued by train to Mashhad, crossed over into Afghanistan, and embarked on a gruelling 24-hour bus ride to Kabul, during which I had my first chillum of black Afghan. Man, Afghanistan was wild, the land, the people, everything. I loved it. There were literally thousands of people on the move along that route to India, hippies, backpackers, students, going or coming. Kabul was one of the places that was very popular as a rest stop along the way. I ended up staying there for a few weeks, and also went for a trip up into the mountains, to the ancient Buddha statues of Bamiyan and to those beautiful deep blue lakes of Band-i-Amir.

Eventually, I decided to move on, together with a high school friend I'd run into on a street in Kabul. I crossed the Khyber Pass into Pakistan, and on August 5 finally made it into India. By the time I had made it across the border near the town of Ferozepur, it was dark, and I got on a bicycle rickshaw to take me there. We moved along a dark Indian country road that was bordered by mysterious swamps, listening to the cacophony of the frogs that lived there. There was a full moon hanging in the sky, and the air was heavy with the sweet smell of jasmine and what not else. And deep down inside, maybe faint, but still so much present that I couldn't help noticing, I had a feeling of coming home. I went as far as Delhi and Agra, and realized that at that point India was a bit too much of a bite for me to swallow. But I knew that I would be coming back someday for more.

***

-3-

The trips during those years were perhaps the best ones that I ever went on. Everything was new to me, and there was a whole world out there to discover. In the following summer, Africa was the next goal I picked. I flew to Cairo, took a good look around Egypt, and in Aswan got on a boat to take me along Lake Nasser to Wadi Halfa in Sudan. It was July, and blistering hot. On the boat, my fellow travelers and I started to fantasize about getting us a cool beer from the tap once we'd arrive. No such luck. Wadi Halfa consisted of a few forlorn small mud and brick buildings in the middle of the desert, a few miles from the lake, and the only thing available was hot tea or lukewarm bottles of Fanta. We had to wait around half a day, which didn't do much to raise our spirits, until we embarked on a 36-hour train trip that would bring us to Khartoum. We were traveling fourth class, since that was the cheapest, and the train was so packed that we were practically sitting on top of each other, together with the locals and their goats and chickens. Outside, nothing but desert. The nights were a bit of a relief, and we climbed on top of our railroad car to spend the time there in the cool breeze.

In Khartoum, it took me a couple of days to get the necessary papers, permits and tickets together for my further trip up the Nile, and I got a good taste of a corrupt and inefficient bureaucracy at work. It was another 12-hour train ride south to Kosti, from where it went on by boat. In effect, it was four sizable steamers, crowded as seemed to be the local custom, and tied together with two in front and two in the back, that were slowly laboring up the river. And I was traveling deck class.

Nobody knew exactly how long it would take to reach Juba, our destination way down in southern Sudan, close to the Ugandan border. Slowly, the landscape changed from monotonous desert to monotonous lush green. In the north, the population consisted of Arabs that were Muslims, while in the south it was blacks of a Christian faith that still had a lot of animistic elements. We stopped at one town that had a few small shops where some canned goods could be bought. The other stops were at more or less traditional villages, with the natives still running around in their birthday suits, and the only thing they had to sell was fish and live chickens. The food that could be bought on the boats was very basic, at the most, and by the time we reached Juba after 10 days I'd had pretty much enough of the Sudan. Sure, today I look back at that trip in a more romantic and nostalgic way, but at that time all I could think of was to get the fuck out of there. So I did just that and within a couple of days managed to get on an Air Sudan flight bound for Entebbe, Uganda.

Talking with some of the other passengers on the flight, I first heard of a guy named Idi Amin, who was running Uganda and was supposed to be rather crazy, and that not in the positive sense of the word. In fact, he was a total crackpot, and I soon was to find out about some of the side effects of his rule.

Upon arrival at Entebbe, I was told at immigration that unless I shaved off my beard I'd be taking the next plane out of the country.

Apparently hippies were not very welcome, and if you happened to have a beard, that made you one. I did manage that shave, somehow, and proceeded to Kampala, where I just wanted to take a breather and eat some decent food.

And yes, thrown in as a bargain, during a stroll through town I managed to catch a glimpse of The Man. In a small park, standing on a low podium and surrounded by a sizable crowd, there was none other than Idi Amin, with a revolver on each hip, giving a speech. However, I felt it would be better to keep a low profile, disappeared around the next corner and went back to my hotel. The next day, I left Kampala to take a look around the country.

Uganda is a very pretty country, with an amazing wildlife that can be seen just from a passing car. I still have that picture of myself sitting on the equator, with one half of my rear end in the northern hemisphere, the other half in the southern. The people were friendly, if a bit naive - they didn't appear to be as sophisticated as the Indians I had encountered the year before.

It was mainly whites that I hitched rides with that were telling me all kinds of stories about what was going on in the country, and I started to get a bit concerned. A lot of people were disappearing mysteriously, dead bodies were dumped into the Nile by the truckload, and the army was manning the border posts to Kenya. If they felt like it, they helped themselves to the valuables of people leaving the country. Maybe I should have taken that "next plane out" after all, but it was too late. Here I was, and I had to face the facts.

Back in Kampala, I met Marvee, an Australian who felt in a similar way, and he had an idea. Situated right on the border to Kenya was Mt. Elgon, an ancient, long extinct volcano, all of 14,178 feet (4321 m) high. Supposedly it was a very nice hike if you went up in Uganda, crossed the border at the top, and then went down to Kenya. "Sounds like a good plan," I said, and off we went.

We hitchhiked as far as we could, and then took a taxi until we reached the end of the road in a small village. We had figured that it would take us three to four days to cross the mountain, and with our last Ugandan shillings bought a bit of food at a local grocery store, then left the village on a dirt track that seemed to be heading where we wanted to go. A local policeman came running after us, trying to tell us that we couldn't go further up, but we didn't bother. We went on up, and up, and up.

We met the last people we'd see for the next few days during the morning of the second day - some tribesmen on the hunt with bow and arrow (no kidding). Around noon on the third day we reached the top, or rather, the crater. Most of the vegetation had by now disappeared, and up there only grass and some strange looking larger plants were in residence. The crater was a few miles wide, and while we were crossing it, it started to rain, hard, and soon we were soaked. Luckily enough, we found a small cave a ways down on the other side, where we made a fire and spent a very cozy night.

We couldn't really get lost, we just had to keep on in a generally eastern direction, heading down now. Up to then, for most of the time, we'd had some kind of a path. Then, during the morning of the fourth day, we came into an area inhabited by wild elephants. Parts of the forest were smashed to pieces, as if a hurricane had gone through it, and we lost our path. We actually saw some of the elephants, stomping around in the jungle maybe a hundred yards off. For the next day and a half there was no path in sight, and that was a very hard piece of work. We had practically no food left, our bodies were pretty sore by now, and all we could do was to plod on, from sunrise until it got dark at night.

Late on the fifth day we found a path that we could follow. That path became wider, and at some point during the sixth day a clearing in the forest opened up in front of us, with a small maize field and a hut in which some solitary local guy was living. He saw us coming out of the forest and probably thought we had come from some different planet, but we just went up to him and said, "Man, you can't imagine how good it is to see you!" He couldn't speak any English, but showed us the way to a dirt road that led to a small settlement a few more miles onwards. There was a shop there that, besides household goods, was selling Coca Cola and candy, and I can't remember that stuff ever tasting better. We were too wiped out to go on any further, so we just sat by the side of the road until a car came by that took us to the next town.

A couple of days later I met a backpacker in the Nairobi Youth Hostel who showed me the current issue of Time Magazine. It featured an article about the situation in Uganda, along with a picture of several people in what appeared to be a dark prison cell, subtitled, "The dark hole of Kampala". "Look," he said, "that's me," pointing at one of the persons. Dang, I was sure glad I'd gotten out of there with my hide intact, and, to boot, made it through a nice little adventure that I'll be able to tell my grandchildren about. (I very much doubt that I'll ever have any, but I still like that line, and so I put it here.)

The rest of the trip was almost a bit anticlimactic. I went around Kenya and Tanzania, saw some stunning vistas and some very monotonous ones, visited a few national parks with an amazing wildlife, and finished off with a trip up the coast, from Dar-Es- Salaam to Malindi. In early October I caught a charter flight back to London.

It had been some journey, almost an explorer trip, considering that I didn't know where I'd be going when I got off the plane in Cairo, other than a very general idea. Still, all in all, I was left with a feeling that was difficult to put a finger on. It wasn't frustration, but rather a sense that something had been missing, that deep down I had been searching for something that I didn't manage to find. In due time, I was going to get the answer to that one, and I would need to cover a few more miles until then.

***

-4-

In the spring of 1973, I went on a tour that brought me to Cyprus and several Greek islands, all very pretty, but I came home with a similar feeling as after my trip to Africa ... was I really looking for something else?

During most of the summer of that year, I was busy doing some practical work for my university studies. However, I noticed that at the end of the summer vacation I'd be able to squeeze in a six week trip before classes resumed in the fall. The hell with it, I said to myself, I'm going back to India.

I flew to Bombay, and the moment I stepped off the plane I knew this was it. Within hours I was on a southbound train, just totally in the groove. I visited the temples of Belur, Somnathpur and Madurai, I went on a mind-blowing boat trip through the backwaters of Kerala, I hopped over to Ceylon for a week, I was awed by places like Mahabalipuram and Tiruchirapalli, where just the name alone was sounding like music in my ears, and I hung out on the beach in Goa.

Yeah, this was my honeymoon with India, and, as we know, when you're in love you don't see any of the pimples that might be there, or they don't seem to matter. Sure, I was smoking plenty of pot along the way, but that wasn't the only thing that got me high. Rather, there was a subtle vibe in the land, the ancient temples, in the way that the Indians were living, some kind of a remnant of India's glorious spiritual past, a lingering fragrance of all the Buddhas that have walked there in times long gone. Something in me picked up on that energy, and I was deeply touched by it. All I could think of now was to get back there as soon as possible.

In effect, it was almost a year and a half before I could set out again. This time I spent several weeks in Nepal, visited Varanasi and, before going home, places in Orissa. I experienced some of the most magical times ever at the Sun Temple of Konarak, which to this day remains my favorite place in India.

In August 1976 I went back to Nepal and lived for several months in the small village of Bodhnath, a few miles outside Kathmandu. At university, I had been studying geography, specializing in regional planning and the Indian subcontinent. In Bodhnath, I did research for my MA thesis on the "socio-economic structure and development of a Nepalese pilgrimage village".

All in all, I've had a lot of fun during my years as a student, with plenty of sex, drugs and rock & roll. But I also went through two periods, lasting for months altogether, where I was feeling very depressed. I indulged in meditating on negative thoughts, lost all perspective on life and did not know how to deal with it psychologically.

By chance, just recently I came across a book on Auroville that my girlfriend at the time had given to me as a birthday present back in 1977. The note she had written in it reflected a bit of concern for the somewhat troubled young man I must have been then. While I was putting the final touches on my MA thesis, I was dreaming of living in Auroville and smoking a lot of dope, but was obviously having difficulties to get it all straight in my head, what I wanted from life and what it was all about. Although I was able to see that I was being pulled by different, opposing forces into different directions, I did not have the clarity at the time to really identify them, nor the integrity to balance them out.

True, I had never really known what I wanted to do in life, no "great master plan". Going to university and traveling had created a diversion for a while, but if you're honest with yourself, you can fool yourself only for so long. Now, my time as a student was winding down, and I was confronted with the necessity of deciding in which direction I wanted to continue.

***

PART II:

POONA

-5-

Meanwhile, back in India, an enlightened mystic started to do his thing ...

On March 21, 1974, the 21st anniversary of his enlightenment, Osho, then known as Bhagwan Shree Rajneesh, moved to Poona. In Koregaon Park, an upscale residential area on the outskirts of town, four adjoining plots comprising of a total of six acres (2.4 hectares) had been bought that were to evolve into the famed Shree Rajneesh Ashram.

By then, Osho had already established a reputation for himself as the most radical and controversial guru on the scene in India. Until 1966, he had been a professor at the University of Jabalpur, teaching philosophy. After resigning from his post he spent several years of intense traveling throughout India. In 1970 he settled in Bombay and started to give regular discourses to the small group of spiritual seekers that had formed around him. In September of the same year, he initiated his first disciples into sannyas, which can be seen as the link between master and disciple. But while the traditional Indian concept of sannyas is more directed towards a renunciation of the world, his "neo-sannyas" was to be a renunciation of the ego, the conditioned mind. A significant part of the game was that at the initiation, the disciples ("sannyasins") received a new name that was preceded by the title "swami", for the men, and "ma", for the women, and from now on they were to wear only orange-colored clothes and the *mala*, a necklace of wooden beads.

The move to Poona set the stage for arguably the most significant experiment of the 20th century to transform human consciousness on a large scale. Here, spiritual seekers were given the opportunity to "work on their issues" in a way that went far beyond listening to Osho's morning discourses or attending *darshan* in the evening. Meditations, therapy groups, bodywork sessions, individual counselling sessions, meditation camps and more provided a complementary framework to Osho's vision, through which visitors were able to existentially experience what this was all about.

Besides the seekers that came for a few weeks or months and then went back "home", an increasing number felt a deeper commitment to stay on indefinitely. After "doing groups" for a while, the next level of involvement was to work at the Ashram, which in itself was a multidimensional spiritual therapy.

By the late seventies, the number of visitors was turning more and more into an avalanche. Thousands were coming to Poona from all over the world. Hotels and private places where they could stay within easy commuting distance to the Ashram were becoming very rare. Hundreds of people were working at the Ashram, and the space for working and living became increasingly cramped. External properties needed to be rented to facilitate the growing need for accommodation and facilities. In 1980, it was estimated that there were between five and seven thousand people in and around the Ashram at any given time. All this certainly added to the pressure-cooker intensity of life at the Ashram itself, but much of the energy was being diluted because a considerable part of virtually everybody's life was taking place in an Indian city that was just outside the gate.

Around that time, Osho started talking about a "new commune", the next phase of his work, with its own land and buildings, a bit more separate from "the world" than the way things were at present. The question was, where. A number of attempts were made to find a suitable place in India, without success, largely because the Indian government looked anything but favorably at the activities of the Ashram.

On June 1, 1981, Osho flew to the United States to seek medical treatment for his back problems. A short time afterwards Rajneesh Foundation bought the Big Muddy Ranch, a former cattle ranch located in the high desert of central Oregon. Consisting of about 125 square miles (324 square kilometers - that's about twice the size of either the District of Columbia, or of the Principality of Liechtenstein), the property was badly overgrazed. Where once tall grasses had grown in abundance, there were now just tufts of short grass, sagebrush and occasional juniper trees.

When Osho arrived in late August, reportedly one of his first remarks was, "Where are all the trees?" What was also lacking was housing, since the original ranch buildings consisted of nothing more than a few small farmhouses and sheds.

***

-6-

And at some point along the way, I started to enter into the picture ...

When I first arrived in Poona in November 1977, I did not have much of a clue of what was going on at the Ashram. Sure, I was a spiritual seeker of sorts, but pretty much in my head about it and quite frustrated about the answers I was getting to my questions in the milieu I'd been living in. I was 29 years old and I'd just finished university, and the only thing I felt like doing was to go back to India. This time, however, whether it was really clear to me or not, I was looking for spiritual guidance, but I did not quite know how to go about to find it, at least on a conscious level.

So when a friend who had given me a ride to the airport had suggested to look up "Rajneesh in Poona" - "He's a good guru, go and see him!" - it had sounded like a fair enough idea to check the place out for a couple of days. And so it came about that two weeks later, on a bright and sunny morning, I found myself and my backpack in front of the Ashram gate. Fortunately, I didn't run away (nor, for that matter, did I ever really leave from there, either).

I immediately liked the sannyasins. They were quite a cool bunch of people, loose and natural, and I felt very comfortable among them. I also was very much interested in the program that the Ashram was offering. Right on the day of my arrival I went to the Ashram office to book a few groups, and started participating in the meditations.

It took me a little longer to find out what was going on with the guy with the long beard and the white robe who was obviously at the center of things (and I can't say that I've ever really gotten to the bottom of that, not to this day). Supposedly, he was "enlightened", and nothing in my life had prepared me for such an encounter, even less so with a high-caliber master like him.

It wasn't until I opened up a bit more and started to become sensitive to the energy field that surrounded him, an energy that permeated everything in and around the Ashram and that became stronger the closer I got to him physically, that something started to click. In a way, the energy was like a beautiful drug that hung there in the air and just needed to be breathed in to get me on a really nice high, at times more mellow, at other times so strong that it seemed to overwhelm me. And besides just feeling good, there were side effects that could be of immense help for a seeker on the path. It added a great amount of clarity to anything I'd focus on, and when I'd close my eyes and start groping around inside, all of a sudden walls and barriers disappeared that had been there before. It was this energy that was giving a different meaning, a whole new dimension to everything that was happening at the Ashram, and to be perceptive to it was the key to at least to begin to understand what was going on there.

***

-7-

Within a few days after my arrival the groups started that I had booked, and slowly, but surely life at the Ashram started to swallow me up. After a couple of introductory groups, Centering and Enlightenment Intensive, the "Tao" group began, and I got a hands-on taste of what is commonly known among sannyasins as "working on your shit".

During those days, a few of the groups held at the Ashram included an open expression of physical violence, and that could not only be directed against a pillow in the corner, but against other group participants as well. We were not supposed to hurt each other, so the group leader had to be absolutely on top of the situation. Since this was happening in Osho's energy field, the group leaders could use that as a support and by far exceed the limitations that they would have had with their normal professional expertise. Still, occasionally someone did get hurt, and those people could be seen hanging out on the Zen Wall (a low wall that ran from near the main gate to opposite Lao Tzu gate) or in the smoking temple, showing off the casts on their arms or legs.

The most famed (and feared) group of this genre was the "Encounter" group, lead by Teertha (Paul Lowe), who had been a therapist of rank and name back in England before becoming a sannyasin. Generally, he was seen as Osho's chief disciple, and in accordance with that he moved around the Ashram in a very dignified manner. In discourse, he had his customary seat in the center of the first row, right in front of Osho, it was him that read out the sutras at the beginning of the discourse, and many of us thought that he was "almost enlightened". In any case, he was one hell of a good group leader, notwithstanding of what might have become of him later on. The Ashram prided itself to be offering the "toughest encounter group in the world", and, even in a buddhafield, this needed a very capable guy to run it.

"Tao", now, was one of "those" groups. During the first session the eighteen of us were sitting in a circle, with the group leader, a gnarled, woodsman-type Californio named Amitabh in the center, and I can still hear his opening remarks, "Guys, everybody here is fucked up, and I'm the most fucked up - that's why I'm the group leader!" And off we went. There was a considerable amount of fighting and screaming (the Germans really went for it there; for them, it was constantly "Scheisse, Scheisse!"), but we also had more quiet sessions with subtle energy work.

There was a Swiss lady who was so much of a case that she had to be exorcised, and there was this cute chick from Munich who had such a hate-thing going on with me that a few times, ignited by a remark or a grin from me, she came charging right across the room in an attempt to tear my eyes out. (Eventually, Amitabh "turned" her, and we became good friends, for many years.) What was quite an interesting revelation to me was that, with the kind help of the other participants, I became acquainted with somebody I had not dared to be confronted with before, had hardly known he existed in the first place: Bodhena, the asshole. Hm!

All in all, I finished the group somewhat wiser, with a cracked rib (that was re-cracked in another group a few weeks later), and I was so hoarse from screaming that I was barely able to whisper.

Within a short time, the groups, together with Dynamic and Kundalini, Osho's classic active meditations, began to show their effect. Most notably, there was an incident when I was having an argument with some lady at the apartment I was sharing with a few other sannyasins. All of a sudden, I felt this surge of energy rising up from my belly, an energy I had never felt before. Wow, it looked like I was now capable to *really* get angry, and not only be in my head about it. Now, that's what I call progress!

After all, group leaders at the Ashram claimed that in this environment within a short time therapeutic successes could be achieved that would take months or even years under more "normal" circumstances. It was the combination of therapy and meditation, plus Osho's energy and guidance that did the trick. For starters, a lot of garbage was thrown out that had collected over years, over lifetimes. There is nothing wrong to get a dysfunctional ego back into whack, but this was not where the work stopped, this was where it really began for Osho. He once said that "you may think you've come here for your problems, but I'm cooking something else." And *what* that is, I am still continuing to discover today.

***

-8-

During my first weeks in Poona, I didn't get to see very much of Osho. Back then, he was giving discourses alternately in Hindi and in English, for a month at a time, starting on the 11th of each month. I had arrived during a "Hindi month", so it wasn't until December 11 that I was treated to my first live English discourse. (Then, his words had still been more important to me than his presence.) This day also happened to be Osho's birthday, and many sannyasins had come to Poona for that occasion to have a big celebration. The discourse series was on Hakuin's "Song of Meditation", and Osho started out with the words, "My beloved ones: I love you. Love is my message ..." Man, that discourse totally knocked me out of my socks, and to this day it remains my absolute favorite. (As for the "Song of Meditation", Osho's present to us on that day, if you're of a mind for a taste, see Appendix "A" at the end of this story.)

From that day on, going to discourse became a regular thing for me; in fact, I started to feel that I was being pulled there like towards a magnet. By the end of the month it also had become clear to me that I could not avoid the question of whether to become a disciple any longer, so I decided to take the jump, and then to just wait and see what this was all about.

On January 6, 1978, Osho initiated me into sannyas. He gave me the name Deva Bodhena, Deva meaning "divine", and Bodhena - derived from the Sanskrit root "bodh" - means awareness, consciousness, as in Buddha or Bodhisattva. "Awareness is the bridge to the divine," he told me, hinting at the nature of my path as a seeker. He continued talking to me for quite a while, of which I don't have very much of a recollection - my mind must have been quite gone.

As an "outside sign" of being a sannyasin, I was now required to wear "orange", which translated into wearing clothes colored in any shade of red. Osho probably has said enough on that subject to fill a whole book. The significance of it I felt most strongly was that it appeared like a simple, but extremely effective device to get thrown back upon myself. Those colors just draw attention, particularly in the West, and there is no place you can hide anymore.

In addition, I had to wear the *mala*, a necklace consisting of 108 wooden beads (that's 2 x 2 x 3 x 3 x 3 - for the numerologists among you) and a "guru bead", a wooden locket with Osho's picture.

The way I had initially looked at that whole issue was that on a woman, the *mala* might look OK, except for that funny locket ("Say, who's *that*? Your favorite movie star?"), but on a man it was looking downright weird - and now I was supposed to run around like that myself! It also had to be worn outside the clothes, not hidden underneath a few layers. And as far as the red-hued clothes went, shit, at least they could have let me keep my blue jeans!

However, it didn't take long to get used to my new "habit", and I especially got a big kick out of wearing my *mala*, I really got hooked. And if somebody out there didn't like it, well, fuck 'em. Moreover, a definite advantage this outfit had was that it made it quite easy to go underground, should that ever be needed - just put on "normal" colored clothes, and you simply disappear.

Incidentally, a few days after I had taken sannyas I had the following dream: I was hanging out on the low wall opposite the main gate, where we'd always take our beedie breaks. Osho came strolling out of the gate and stopped in front of me. He took off his white robe, underneath which he was wearing a three-piece pinstripe suit, and then he flipped me the finger. Now, what could *that* mean? (Your personal koan, swami!)

***

-9-

In many ways, the Ashram was a small universe of its own, with a totally different *modus operandi* than the world just outside the main gate, and with its own very particular jargon. The key word was "energy". It was energy this, energy that, did you feel that person's energy, what is the energy of this moment, my energy is really low today, et cetera. As we all know, energy is not static, it moves, changes, and this happens in a "space". So life at the Ashram was seen as a play of changing energies, happening in different spaces (like in my head, or in the kitchen), and to see that you need consciousness (which, ultimately, was what the place was all about).

The more you were in a state of let-go and not clinging to your mind, the more you could just flow and fly with the whole scene. In that space people were meeting and relating to each other, was the work happening, and you could just watch how things were getting done through you, as a part of a larger entity. Sure, as often is the case, a flow of energy may be blocked, in one way or another, and this is where the therapy groups and the active meditations came in, and, at a later stage, the "work" at the Ashram.

When you were not in tune, you were bumping into so many corners that all you wanted to do was to get out ASAP. This was also the case when you were stoned on ganja, then the Ashram was a place that was better to be avoided. As nice as a doped- up head may feel, this did not jibe with the way the Ashram was operating.

Socially, people were totally respected in their individual spaces, as long as they weren't bugging somebody else. If you wanted to be by yourself, you were left alone. If you wanted to relate, you did that with like-"minded" people, and here the commune consisted of an intricate maze of social in-groups.

If you were an ashramite, you had it made. From what I heard, that also had its price: you got your buttons pushed 24 hours a day, you couldn't just "go home" in the evening like the rest of us. A very cliquish sub-group were the group leaders, who were often seen as demigods by newcomers. Another much envied sub-group consisted of the residents of Lao Tzu House (which was where Osho was living), and of the people working there. By and large, it was those people who had their regular and reserved seats in discourse, closest to Osho. Even among them there was a lot of jockeying going on about who could sit where. One row closer to Osho often made all the difference in somebody's spiritual self- esteem.

Vivek, Osho's personal caretaker, was the one everybody was jealous of. Everybody's first interest was to get as close to Osho as possible, in any way that was possible, the organizational structure around him permitting, and of all people it was Vivek, who by some karmic merits was in the hot seat. As the tale goes, in her previous incarnation she had been a young girl that had been a close friend of Osho when he was a teenager. When she was dying of typhoid, she made Osho promise to call her back in her next life. She was reborn in England, and traveled to India when she was in her early twenties. "Do you remember me?" he asked her when they met in Bombay sometime in the early seventies. Try to match that!

A bit further towards the periphery were the rest of the Ashram workers, but that still came with a lot of perks, depending on how long you had been working, how dedicated a worker you appeared to be in the eyes of the Ashram management, or how well connected you were in general. There was the privilege to sit closer to the front in discourse (behind the "reserved" ones), and the workers even had their own line to wait before discourse, and that line was admitted ahead of the "common" line. A very much desired thing to have was a food pass, which was an issue that was handled quite individually. Still, if you had worked for, say, half a year, you generally got one. Now you could eat for free, and that at Mariam Canteen, the place where all the VIPs ate.

This whole setup was not fixed, it was not like the caste system that was being practised outside the gate. On the contrary, it was very flexible, and a lot depended on where an individual was at energy-wise, or where your luck just took you to. There was this beautiful lady from South America who came to Poona, took sannyas, hooked up with the Ashram stud and instantly became a celebrity, so much so that Osho even mentioned her in discourse.

Understandably, it was the newcomers and the non-sannyasins that were on the bottom rung of the pecking order. I have been told by non-sannyasins that they have often experienced sannyasins as arrogant. Well, what can I say? I have also felt this within the sannyasin community, whether it was in the vibes of some sannyasin bigwigs as they were strutting down the main drag of the Ashram, or in the frown I got from our famous musical *maestro* when he passed me one day while I was sitting at the back gate, strumming my guitar. I guess it is pretty much the same game a twelfth-grader plays with his underclassmen, this I'm-better-than-you-because-I-know-more-than-you kind of an ego trip, and here it came in its spiritual variety. (And the situation certainly gets more interesting if the receiving party suffers from an inferiority complex.)

Like people elsewhere, sannyasins come in two sexes. To be quite frank with you, it would have been rather unnatural if, particularly in that place, I hadn't shown a "certain" interest in the other sex. Good God, in my whole life I have never come across a more stunning collection of beautiful (and, depending on the circumstances, available) females than at the Ashram.

Contrary to what outsiders commonly believed, there was not this big orgy going on, but rather an exploration into sexuality without the taboos and hang-ups that normally go along with it. Ultimately, you got what you brought into the game. Everything was there, from one night stands to deep and meaningful relationships of any duration. I have heard of people that went to Poona just to fuck their brains out. Whether they accomplished that or not, they probably got just what they deserved, but not the real thing. (As the Beatles sing it at the end of Abbey Road - "And in the end, the love you take is equal to the love you make". And that's exactly what it comes down to.)

As far as this here swami went, I had a lot of fun. Those were the days after the pill had been invented, and before the advent of AIDS, and the worst I ever got from it was a few crabs, along with a generous assortment of heart-breaks, feelings of jealousy, possessiveness and whatever else can befall you when you participate in this game.

Sannyasins coming to Poona were not necessarily encouraged to bring their kids along, if they had any. People were supposed to meditate and to work on their stuff, and taking care of kids was seen as creating too much of a distraction from one's own inner processes. However, if they came along anyway, those kids were totally accepted for who they were, and I envied them that so early in their lives they could spend time at a place like the Ashram. Mainly for the kids of ashramites and long-term workers, there was a school at Hem Hira, a property the Ashram had rented.

Everybody's (and Osho's) favorite was little Siddhartha, a young rascal aged maybe seven or eight (difficult to say, because he was really quite an ancient one). Osho often talked about him, and he was frequently seen hanging out in the smoking temple, bumming beedies and change. Alert and centered as he was and with an extraordinary presence, he had the knack of getting what he wanted, and getting away with it. At times, he could be seen packing a big plastic toy gun, and once, together with his pals, he went around the smoking temple, telling everybody present, one after the other, "Go fuck your girlfriend!" This kid was a total riot! From what I heard, he nowadays is a celebrity DJ in Chile. Way to go, Sid!

***

-10-

Meanwhile, it had become more and more clear to me that it was here where I really wanted to be, to devote my time to surrender to what was going on between Osho and me on a deeper level. The last doubts I might have had were dispersed by Somendra (Michael Barnett), with whom I had done a knock-out group called "Leela" later that winter. After the group, I had gone to see him, telling him how I felt about being here with Osho, but that I also had that old dream to go and live in California. "Look," he said, "California is a far out scene which will probably blow your mind, but the people that are ready there, they are coming here!" That did it for me, and I "decided" to make it my first priority to do whatever was humanly possible to be close to Osho, whatever the consequences.

Still, I also had to support myself somehow, for which money was needed. What to do? Then I remembered that my professor at my German university had asked me if I wanted to get into a PhD program, and so I came up with the glorious idea to start writing a doctorate thesis about the Ashram. I sent in a letter to Osho, asking him how he felt about it, and his reply was, "It is a good program, go and do it."

By now, I had been in Poona for almost half a year, after which it was going to be more difficult and costly to obtain a visa extension, so I thought this was an appropriate time to take a bit of a break, go back to the West and do there what needed to be done.

Every evening at seven, Osho was giving *darshan* (Sanskrit, "to see", in its deeper sense) to a small group of disciples and visitors in Chuang Tzu Auditorium, which was adjacent to Lao Tzu House. Here, new disciples were initiated, and during those times the number of visitors to Poona was still so small (relatively), that people could come forward individually and get one-on-one, personal spiritual guidance on almost any given subject, ranging from how things were going with your girl- or boyfriend, to the relationship with your parents, or if there was any problem with your meditation. Also, sannyasins leaving Poona had a "leaving *darshan*", and those coming back got an "arriving *darshan*", during which they could talk with their master face to face.

On May 2, 1978, I had my leaving *darshan*. When it was my turn, I went forward and sat in front of Osho.

"Hello, Bodhena," he said, "when are you leaving?"

"Tomorrow," I replied.

"And when will you be coming back?" he wanted to know.

"If everything goes well, by fall."

And this is where he got me, where just by this small sentence he clearly saw through the way my mind was operating (not that this was anything special, but still).

This was his response:

"By fall? Everything will go well - cross out that 'if'! Never get hooked by 'ifs' and 'buts'. Make life simple, and without 'ifs' and 'buts' life is very simple. 'Ifs' and 'buts' create great complexity. Because we create our life through our thinking: if you say 'if' then there will be an 'if'; you are projecting it. Don't project hesitations. Just say, 'Everything will be well and I will be here by fall' ... and everything will be well; there is no problem in it. Man creates his own world by thinking about it continuously."

And as a farewell present, he gave me one of his "magic boxes", a small wooden box containing one of his hairs. Over the years, it has helped me out of a number of tight spots, in a truly magical way, and still today it remains a good companion.

***

-11-

I returned to Germany just in time to witness the first big press wave on Osho and the Ashram roll off. My parents, who had been quite shocked when I came back in orange and *mala*, now were totally beside themselves. It all had started when in the summer of 1977 Stern, one of the biggest magazines in Germany, had sent one of its star reporters to Poona for three weeks. Jörg Andrees Elten not only went to discourses and took a good look around the Ashram, but also participated in a few groups, most notably in Teertha's Encounter group, and ended up taking sannyas. Now calling himself Swami Satyananda, he had a few problems to get his article published the way he wanted it, but eventually it came out in January 1978. (I remember reading it in the Ashram office, and we were all very excited about it.)

Still, the article had been too positive, too unsensational, and not much happened. What really kicked the whole thing into high gear was this third-rate German movie starlet named Eva Renzi who had come to Poona and supposedly had not been treatedaccording to her expectations in a group she had enrolled in at the Ashram. The German press happily jumped onto that, and by the summer of 1978, the wave was rolling. Just about every magazine on the market as well as many daily papers published reports and articles, and there were mainly two topics that they keyed in on, the liberal attitude towards sex at the Ashram, and the use of violence in a few of the therapy groups there, and all that in the context of a "religious cult" in an exotic environment. Can't get any better! They certainly were not interested in the truth and probably only saw what they were able to see, anyway. Bild, the biggest German daily with a circulation of a few million copies and specializing in bottom drawer stuff, even ran a whole series that went on for over a week, and I have never come across a weirder and more warped fairy tale in my whole life.

All that got my poor parents totally confused now, they didn't know *what* to believe any more. In any case, they were right about one thing, that their son was a goner. And on a larger scale, this put Poona on the map and made Osho a household name throughout Germany. There were a lot of people that did see through the bullshit the press was printing, and in the end it helped bring more people to Poona than ever before.

All in all, things went very smoothly in Germany. No "ifs" and "buts", no problem. I saw Dr. Haffner, my professor at the university, and talked things over with him. He was a very nice and open person who had been to India many times himself (and, to my credit, I must say that he did have some trust in my scientific capabilities). He was game as far as my proposed thesis was concerned, and I also managed to snag a grant that would finance my project for a year (and that could be extended for another one).

So I returned to Poona in the fall and started to look at what was happening at the Ashram with my scientific mind. After all, that was how I had been trained to look at life. This was maybe not exactly the appropriate way to approach a mystery school, but still sufficient for my purposes at the time.

***

-12-

You're probably asking yourself by now what an Ashram has to do with geography. Well, let me tell you this much. The subject of geography is the spatial distribution of phenomena, the patterns they create and their inter-relatedness. These phenomena can be of economic or social nature, or in the field of physical geography, like hydrology or geomorphology. The Ashram as a physical entity was undergoing a very dynamic process which had a definite spatial component, and involved in this were people, whose motivations were putting a certain shape to all this. Of particular interest here was the influence of the Ashram on the city of Poona, and, ultimately, the "new commune" that Osho had been talking about.

Personally, I didn't worry too much about that at the time. I had achieved my main objective, which was that I was back in Poona with the means to support myself, and so I set out to work. The Ashram management was very supportive, as long as I didn't cross certain boundaries. After all, a scientific study like this would only further their own interests, and they knew me well enough to see that they could trust my judgement and that I was not on any negative trip. Still, my first priority was to be a sannyasin, so I did a few more groups and made certain that any research I was involved in wasn't interfering with going to discourse in the morning, doing Kundalini in the afternoon and generally having the social life typical of a sannyasin in Poona.

Ah, those were the days ... just imagine, it is ten in the morning, you are riding high on the energy of yet another beautiful discourse, the sun is shining, the sky has never been more blue (pollution permitting), the trees have never been of a more brilliant green, and the whole world is just waiting to be embraced. You could continue with some more active celebration at Sufi Dancing which by now is getting under way in Buddha Hall, or you could just find your favorite spot on the Zen Wall, watch the river of the Ashram life flow by and wait for something to happen. Invariably, you'd always run into who you needed to meet, maybe a friend who was going back to the West in a couple of days and was going to take along some mail for you, or the beautiful ma you sat next to in discourse the other day, and the outcome might just be that you got yourself a hot date for the evening (or for right there and then).

Before you knew it, it was time for lunch, and afterwards it was over to Buddha Hall for a little nap during the taped discourse. Oops, you almost spaced out that you had to pick up your new *darshan* robe at your tailor, so you'd hop into a rickshaw to MG Road to take care of that, grab a cup of coffee and do a bit of shopping while there, and by the time you were back at the Ashram, Kundalini was about to start.

The place to go to in the evening was Music Group (unless you were one of the lucky ones to have *darshan*). There were hundreds of us there, sometimes up to a thousand, singing and dancing along ("Drinking from your wine, Bhagwan ... "). It was Anubhava, a sannyasin from Germany, who clearly carried the event. Just with his voice and guitar and backed by a few musicians he'd do his magic, every night. There were times the energy was so high that we thought it would lift the roof off Buddha Hall.

As far as food went, we were certainly not starving. There was Vrindavan Restaurant and Snack Bar right at the Ashram, serving a simple and delicious fare suitable for western stomachs, and we could be sure that it had been prepared under the highest hygienic conditions (which was very important if you had arrived in India just recently).

Maybe a fifteen minute walk away was Prem's Restaurant, a place that was very popular among sannyasins (and would continue to be when we'd come back from our American adventure). The place had had its beginnings when a year or two earlier Mr. Prem had rented out a few rooms in his house to sannyasins, and once a week he'd cook dinner for his tenants. Another Indian success story!

If you were on a shoestring budget, you could go for a Club Sandwich at the Cafe Delite (also dubbed "Cafe Disgust"), and for desert head for one of the roadside places across the street from Mobo's Hotel for a mixed fruit pulp, with or without cream (if you didn't specify, you got it "with"). At the Delite, they seemed to be having a persistent shortage of dishes - they always had about a dozen busboys running around the place like bloodhounds ("Finished? Finished?"), and if you didn't hold on to your plate, it was gone, even if you had only eaten half of your meal.

There were a few enterprising sannyasins that were operating restaurants, like the Surrender Garden, a few minutes' walk from the Ashram. The bamboo hut villages that had sprung up on the fields beyond Koregaon Park, along the river, had their own subculture going and also featured a small restaurant here and there.

For the wealthier clientele, there were high-end eateries downtown like the Chinese Room or Latif's, with prices that were still very reasonable by western standards, and not to forget the Hotel Blue Diamond, Poona's only luxury hotel, very conveniently located just around the corner from the Ashram. Its restaurant and bar was a very popular off-hour meeting place for the Ashram establishment.

It was the general hygienic situation in India that created a lot of health problems for western sannyasins. A test conducted by the Ashram laboratory showed that a large percentage of the dust (which was everywhere) consisted simply of shit, and many people came down with dysentery, dengue fever or hepatitis. Also amoebas were quite common, and I've met people who were still battling them years after they had left India.

Fortunately, nothing seemed to touch me. The city water in Poona was supposedly safe, and I drank plenty of it, unboiled. I ate kilos of grapes when they were in season, as well as mangos and apples, without going through an elaborate trip about cleaning them. During the hot season, my favorite was freshly pressed sugarcane juice, with a twist of lemon and ginger and a bit of crushed ice, and believe me, I had countless glasses of that, in a simple shack by the road.

Later that winter it happened that Dr. Weise, the other professor who was overseeing the work on my thesis, came to India on a three week excursion with a group of students. I took a break at the Ashram and tagged along, using my travel expertise to help with the organizing. We went around South India, and also came by Auroville, the spiritual community I had once been interested in. The people there seemed to be nice enough and were living in an admirable fashion, but compared to the intense, high-energy atmosphere of the Ashram that I'd come to know, the place seemed a bit dead. Wearing orange and *mala*, I got a response from some of them to the effect that they appeared to be having a bit of a difficult time coping with the energy of some of Osho's sannyasins they'd met.

At the end of the tour, there were a few days off, and about half of the participants used that time to visit the Ashram, with two of them taking sannyas. A few months later, it was the good professor himself who, along with his young and pretty wife, took the jump. Now going by the name of Swami Devanando, he hung on to his job at the university for another year or so, then dropped out and came back to Poona.

Meanwhile, my research was progressing nicely. I conducted 200 detailed, semi-standardized interviews with Ashram visitors, about where they came from, what they were doing here and what their plans were. One morning before discourse, with a few helpers and generous support from the Ashram management, I handed out short questionnaires to everybody going into Buddha Hall. More than 90% of the questionnaires were returned, almost 1,200. Furthermore, I had in-length interviews with several key persons that gave me a good picture of the organizational structure of the Ashram and of the work happening there, at least the part of it that was visible from the outside. I was also able to use some of the Ashram's own data, as well as a number of the Ashram's publications.

***

-13-

The outcome of the research gave me a pretty good picture of who was here, at least statistically. According to my "discourse survey", the average age was 31 years. The largest age group was the one from 26 to 30 years, with 36%. Another 21% were between 21 and 25 years old, and 30% between 31 and 40. So, by and large, these were the Baby Boomers, the generation that had grown up with Bob Dylan and the Beatles, and who was here were the ones that hadn't given up their quest for the truth yet, that were not satisfied with the dreams promised by the bourgeois society they'd grown up in, however much they might have rebelled against it at some time.

As far as their countries of origin were concerned, the Germans were the strongest national group with almost 20%, followed by the US Americans and the British with a bit over 16% each. Australians, Indians and Dutch accounted for between 6 and 7% each, and Canadians, French and Italians for between 4 and 5% each. Of the remaining 14%, almost 9% came from various other European countries, 3% came from Asia, 1% from Latin America and 0.5% from Africa. Another 1% came from New Zealand, boy, those Kiwis almost fell through the cracks! And in fairness to the Indians I have to add that they were very much underrepresented since their visiting pattern to Poona differed decidedly from the rest.

Professionally and socially, people came from all walks of life. Most of them had had a rather extensive education. Of the 200 visitors I had interviewed, almost 60% had spent at least some time at college or university. I have met, among others, university professors, psychologists, MDs, lawyers, architects, teachers, managers, book keepers, engineers, craftsmen, various kinds of artists, policemen, nurses, secretaries, stewardesses, housewives, students, and quite a few drop-outs. I have also met several people with a rather extensive background in drugs, some of them clean now, some not. And a good friend of mine even confided in me that he'd once robbed a bank - that impressed me, since I agree with Bertold Brecht that founding a bank is a greater crime than robbing one.

There were also the occasional VIPs visiting the Ashram, some more, some less "important". Back in 1977, the singer Diana Ross and Werner Erhard (of EST) had come, and even talked to Osho in *darshan.* Around the same time, the then fairly well-known actor Terence Stamp had taken sannyas, as had Richard Price, one of the founders of the Esalen Institute (he got a bit scared, though, and subsequently backed off). Vinod Khanna, one of the most popular movie stars of the Bollywood scene, had joined the club, too, and did a lot of very positive PR work for Osho. And from time to time, the rumor would go around the Ashram that George Harrison was on his way, who, unfortunately, never made it - apparently he was quite happy with the Hare Krishna.

In 1978, I briefly shared a room with Martin Siems, a psychologist and sociologist who had co-authored the book "Anleitung zum sozialen Lernen" (Instructions for Social Learning), a renowned bestseller at the time in Germany. A few years earlier, I had participated in a "self-help group" (a group run by its participants) with 8 other people that had been based on that book and, for all of us, had been very successful. Martin participated in several groups, and maybe a year later I came across a very positive magazine article he had written about his experiences.

We also had royalty living right among us. Swami Vimalkirti, aka Prince Welf of Hanover, was the great-grandson of the last German emperor. Now he was living at the Ashram with his wife Turiya, an established therapist, and their seven-year-old daughter Tanya. His occupation was that of being a guard at Lao Tzu House. (In January 1981, Vimalkirti suffered a brain hemorrhage during karate training, and died a few days later. His body was brought to Buddha Hall and, with all of us present, Osho came to Buddha Hall and in a very moving gesture touched Vimalkirti's third eye. The body was then brought to the nearby burning ghats by the river for a celebration, with all the sannyasins singing and dancing around the funeral pyre.)

And there were all kinds of deadbeats, pot-heads, weirdoes and crazies hanging out around the fringes of the sannyasin scene in Poona. Some of them had at some point taken sannyas, but more or less dropped it; a few had even gotten their *malas* confiscated. They'd get together at more seedy establishments like the Cafe Bund or the Sunder Lodge, smoking it up. Man, you could go up to the back porch of the Sunder Lodge at almost any time of the day and there'd be a fat joint going around. Actually, there were quite a few sannyasins who still liked to turn on, and this was one of the places to go to score a tola of Manali or some good Kerala grass.

For people with certain psychological conditions it was a risky thing to engage in the activities at the Ashram. Some of them had ignored the advice to return to their home countries, but had stayed around and now were occasionally seen walking around Koregaon Park in a more or less confused state of mind. A few had gone off the deep end, wound up in the local loony-bin across the river and had to be bailed out by their embassies (who were not very pleased about that, as you can imagine).

At the guards department of the Ashram, we had a whole "cuckoo album" of such people that were "banned", complete with mug shots and background stories, and the guards at the gate had to be alert, because sometimes one of those people would try to sneak in and be of a nuisance (like making a big scene and demanding to see Osho).

***

-14-

By the time the first monsoon rains started to fall in the summer of 1979, I had come to a point where it was getting obvious that I needed to start evaluating the data I had collected, so that I could see what I had and how I was going to continue. I flew to Germany, touched base with Dr. Haffner and worked my tail off to put all my findings into a readable and systematic form, a kind of a preliminary study. After three months, I was done and went back to Poona.

When I entered the group booking office upon my return, the lady there greeted me with something like, "Come on, swami, how much longer are you gonna be doing groups?" Well, I had come to that conclusion myself by then, so I booked only one group, the only one that was really left for me to do, a ten-day Vipassana retreat. I totally loved that one, and when it was over, I did not want to leave ... still, I had to face reality.

If I'd had any doubts about my research up to then, they had not been significant, and I had not spent much time contemplating that subject during my retreat. But now it became very clear to me that the work on my thesis did not only appear rather pointless, but that it also had grown more into a barrier that kept me from what I really wanted, which was to become a more integral part of what was happening around Osho.

Within a few days after the group had ended, I decided to drop the whole thing and start working at the Ashram, a step that now had become inevitable. I knew there was a back door open if I ever wanted to continue with my project, but it is not that I had to put it there, or that it played any role in my decision. I have never looked back, and never had any regrets.

***

-15-

In most instances we did not have much of a choice where we were put to work. There was only one way to approach this issue, and that was to have no expectations, and it was helpful if you were finished with any kind of trip that might keep you from putting all of your energy into the work. The word of the moment was "surrender", and a major lesson we were learning was to see to which extent our attitudes were a hindrance to just seeing things as they were, and how they were causing a lot of suffering. If a floor needs to be swept, then it is up to me whether I go through hell while I am doing it, or whether I just enjoy it.

Somehow or other, everybody got the job he or she needed, and if you were wise enough, you trusted that. "In this place, there are no accidents," as I heard one of the group leaders put it. In some cases, people got jobs that were right in line with whatever skills they had, and those egos were fed and polished until they sparkled. In other cases, highly accomplished professionals were given work that had not the least thing to do with what they'd been doing before. The classic example here were the PhDs that were scrubbing the public toilets at the Ashram. This really happened, I've seen those guys as they were happily and lovingly doing their toilet cleaning meditation, and not just for a couple of days. Some of them were doing it for months.

Over the years, the number of workers at the Ashram had been growing steadily, and by the spring of 1979 there were more than 800 of them. (Within the next two years, that number would again grow by about half as many.) Some of them worked only for a duration of a few weeks or months, but many were committed to being in Poona "forever", or were at least here for an open- ended stay. Among them were 300-some ashramites, the rest of them were living outside the premises and were maintaining their own living quarters.

A typical work day started half an hour after morning discourse and went until about 6 pm, with an hour for lunch and a tea-break in the afternoon. There were no days off. The work that needed to be done at the Ashram was done exclusively by sannyasin workers; Indian outside workers were hired only rarely.

Within another year, the "supply", the number of sannyasins at work, started to exceed the "demand", the amount of work that was there to be done. So, in order to accommodate everybody, the Ashram started to give one day a week off to all the workers. I have met people who had worked there for years, without any breaks, and who were totally blown away by having all of a sudden so much personal time for themselves.

So, there were hundreds of people working on just those six acres, and that under high-energy conditions - you can imagine that the Ashram was literally a beehive of activity. And if you consider that the 1.5 acre plot where Lao Tzu House was located was an area accessible to only relatively few people, that increases the density even more. The question is, what were all those people doing?

The basic purpose of the Ashram was to make Osho's teachings, his vision, available to as many people as possible. This was his Ashram, and, ultimately, he called the shots. "This is not a democracy," he once remarked. Most of the day-to-day business was handled by disciples who were seen as capable to do so, to act as his extended arm, as vehicles for his energy, but many things were subject to his direct approval, sometimes down to minor details as to which picture to use for a book cover. Ma Yoga Laxmi, his secretary, would go in and see him on a daily basis for advice and guidance on how to run the show. Nevertheless, the way the Ashram evolved was determined by what *we* needed for our spiritual growth, and this came as a reflection from *him*. He decided what to use, and how, for our benefit.

All this had to be organized, and that it was, in the form of a charitable trust ("Rajneesh Foundation"), responsible largely for running the therapy groups and meditations, and a nonprofit company ("Rajneesh Foundation Limited") that was more or less taking care of the media work, books, audio tapes, etc. It was Laxmi who was "managing trustee" for the former as well as "managing director" for the latter.

In mid-1979, there were a total of 40 different groups being offered at the Ashram, most of them for 14 to 18 participants, and most of them lasting between 3 and 5 days, a few up to 10 or 14 days. Almost all of the groups were offered several times a month. In May 1979, the number of places offered in the groups totaled about 1,850 (half a year earlier, it had been a third less). The groups were always booked up, sometimes one or two months in advance.

For this to happen, a considerable amount of planning and coordination was necessary. If you were a prospective group participant, there were people you could go and see for deciding which groups were advisable for you, and you'd go to the group booking office to sign up and pay for them. The prices were extremely reasonable, typically between 150 and 500 rupees, depending on the duration of the group (then, one US$ would get you 8 rupees at the bank, one DM half as much). And, lastly, at the beginning of each session you would find the group room clean and tidy. Things were being done very professionally, and a lot of work went into all this that was not visible to the normal participant.

The other major area of work was the publishing of Osho's books, mostly verbatim transcripts of his discourses, and, to a lesser degree, transcripts of the evening *darshans*. During those years, about 40 new books were published annually by the Ashram, most of them in English, the rest in Hindi. Most of them were hardcover deluxe editions (several of them had won prizes for their design, in India as well as abroad), with 5,000 copies each. In mid-1979, there were about 340,000 books stored in the "Vipassana Godown", the large storage space near the Ashram back gate, and every month about 10,000 of them were being shipped out.

To do this work, there were editors, proofreaders, typists and translators; we had a dark room where the layout, graphics and photographic work was being done, and in our silk screen-printing department the covers were printed. Only the actual printing and binding of the books were contracted out.

The books could be bought at the Ashram bookshop, along with audio cassettes of the discourses and music by sannyasin musicians, produced by our own tape department. In late 1978, the Ashram started to explore yet another medium by videotaping Osho's discourses. At first this was done only occasionally, and by early 1981 had been expanded to the point that, typically, every other question of the Q&A discourses was taped.

By 1979, about 15 of Osho's books were also published in licensed editions by American and British publishers, and more than 20 of them had been translated and published by German, Dutch, Danish, Italian, French, Spanish, Portuguese and Japanese publishers.

And then, a lot of mouths had to be fed. In charge of the Ashram kitchen was Deeksha, a "beautiful Italian mama", as Osho had called her. A lot of people had a bit of a problem with her, since she also had the temper to go with that attribute. Still, in mid-1979 the one hundred-odd kitchen workers cranked out meals for about 500 people at Mariam (for ashramites and food pass holders), and, at Vrindavan, about twelve hundred meals, two thousand snacks and several thousand cups of beverages, every day. As even the Indian press noted, the kitchen was "sparkling clean" (although otherwise they were a bit stingy in showering us with too many compliments).

The Ashram also had its own health center, staffed (at that time) by 6 MDs and a number of nurses, cleaners, laboratory- and administrative personnel. The ailments most commonly in need of treatment were "the shits" and related diseases, but at the center they were also equipped and capable to do things like minor surgery or gynecological routine jobs. The health center was supplemented by a ward for about a dozen patients and a small pharmacy.

Operating independently from the health center was a fully equipped dental office, run by Devageet, an English dentist who was to rise to fame in later years as Osho's personal dentist. (It was said, though, that his fillings were of the same transient quality as everything else in life …)

In the southwestern corner of the Ashram the carpentry shop was located, which was referred to as the "*Mala* Shop". About 50 people were working there, manufacturing not only the *malas* that Osho gave out to new sannyasins every evening, but also all kinds of furniture needed by the Ashram and, on an experimental basis, wood carvings, musical instruments, jewelry work etc. Very much emphasis was put into quality, because, as Asheesh, the coordinator of the *Mala* Shop explained, "Quality has a cleanliness, a purity in it which helps meditation."

Any construction or repair jobs were done by the 30 or 40 Ashram handymen, capable of just about anything in the field of carpentry, plumbing, cement- and electrical work.

Furthermore, we … Jesus, is this getting too boring? Sorry, I was getting a bit carried away. See, I'm sitting on all those important and interesting findings from my research, and I thought I could sneak in a few tidbits, for your exclusive reading pleasure, and I haven't even gotten to tell you about Venu Boutique, the pottery, the weavery, the gardeners and all the pencil pushers in the offices. But there is one group of people that deserves at least an honorary mention: all those cleaners, who tirelessly swept, scrubbed and dusted and made the Ashram what it was, an oasis of cleanliness in the midst of filthy India. Good work!

***

-16-

I started to work as a handyman for the group department. We were about seven or eight swamis in our crew, and our job was to maintain the group facilities, doing minor carpentry, painting, repairs. Our base was at "Number 70", a rented property which was about a five minute walk from the Ashram. Underneath some trees we had our work benches, tool lockers, our supply of wood and paints and whatever else we needed.

In addition to the group rooms at the Ashram, groups were held at about six different locations, in various rented buildings in or near Koregaon Park, so we were moving around quite a bit. A paint job here, installing new electrical wiring there, building some shoe shelves for this location or some file boxes for the main group office, we were kept pretty busy.

The work was somewhat of a challenge for me since I had practically no prior experience in that field. The learning process I went through went on (at least) on two levels. I was acquiring skills in dealing with all sorts of physical situations that needed to be attended to, with all kinds of different materials and tools, and on a more subtle level I was getting confronted with a lot of the trips I had going on.

A major one for me has always been that it really pisses me off when things aren't working the way they're supposed to by their design. This "design" can be more general, for instance that a saw is there to cut wood, but my own attitudes can add a whole new dimension to it. Moreover, what made things definitely more interesting was that the tools and materials we were working with were "Made in India", which in a lot of cases meant that they were of a rather shoddy quality. And lastly, the buddhafield energy we were working in had the effect to intensify and magnify everything that might be "coming up".

Generally, it wasn't as bad as you might expect. I enjoyed the camaraderie we had going within the crew, and working with my hands certainly helped to get me out of my head. Challenges that were happening along the way were dealt with, sooner or later. Still, there were some instances where through a particular combination of factors I was pushed to my limits, stripped of all my defenses and got totally rattled by the situation. Before I knew what had really happened, I found myself sitting there, sort of looking into a mirror at myself, or rather at whatever was left of it.

One of my most memorable incidents in this regard was an encounter with a folding table. Somebody in our crew had built a small side table that was designed to be affixed to a wall, and was equipped with hinges, so that it would fold down. In the up- position, the table top was held in place by a vertical wooden board underneath that was also hinged to the wall. In order to fold the table down, first you swung the support 90 degrees to the side until it was parallel to the wall, then the top would fold down over it. All this came in one piece, nicely cut, sanded, varnished and screwed together, and I was given the job to go and put it up.

So, on this one fine morning, our young and aspiring handyman took the folding table, an electric drill, some plugs and screws, screwdriver, tape measure, hammer etc. and went to the place where the table was supposed to go up, a small room somewhere in a nearby building. It seemed to be a straightforward job, and I didn't really anticipate any difficulties. However, the deck was stacked against me, and, miraculously, nothing worked.

To start out with, I had a rough time to get the holes drilled into the wall just how and where they needed to be. What certainly helped was the crumbly substance of the wall - I had to abandon a couple of attempts because they were starting to look like craters. By the time I started fiddling around with the plugs my patience had worn a bit thin. And Indian plugs are not those nice plastic jobs that you get in the West. No, they were funny looking short wooden dowels, and there was no way of telling how they would behave once you started to put a screw into them.

I did not give up so easily, though, and kept on laboring and sweating away, without much success, and by and by worked myself into a state where I was, in the end, totally enraged and in tears, feeling utterly helpless and exposed, and at the very end of whatever I knew that I could do to get the job done. The fucking table was still not up, and the scene was looking like a minor disaster area. This was certainly not another example of German engineering and craftsmanship. Crushed, humiliated and defeated, the only thing left for me was to go and get some help. And, as you might or might not have guessed, together with one of the expert carpenters from our crew, it took about ten minutes to complete the job. What a revelation!

***

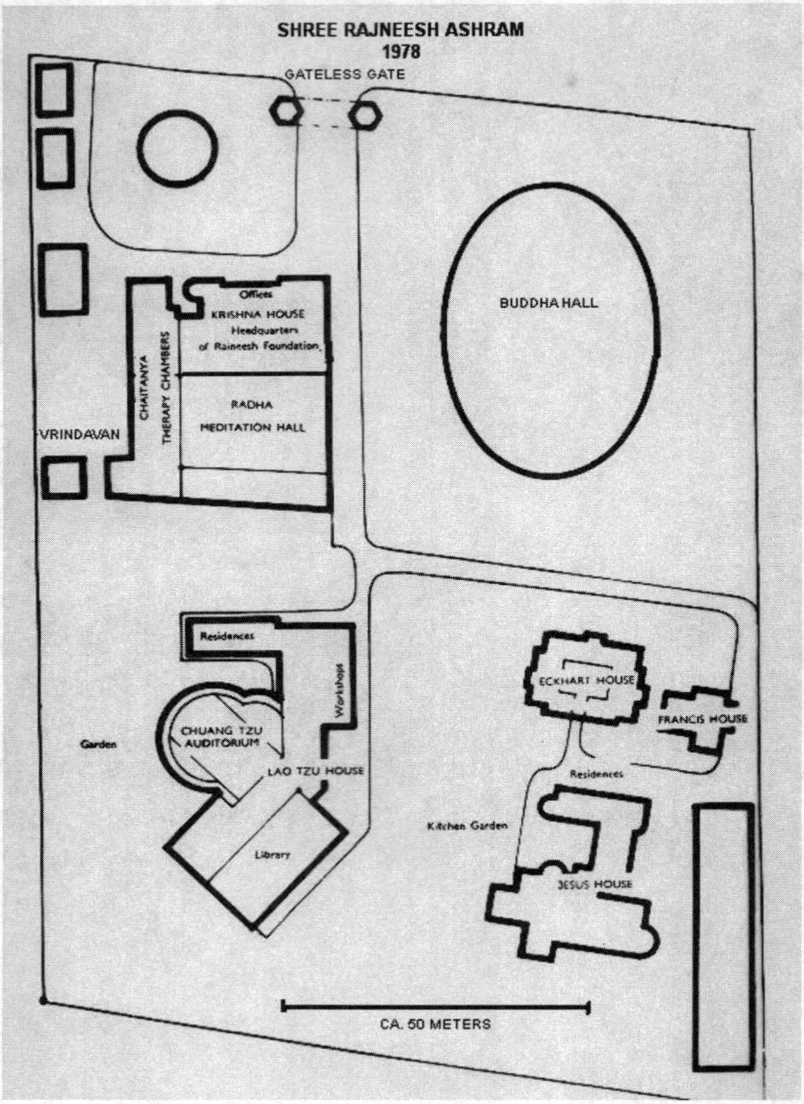

Shree Rajneesh Ashram 1978

The "Gateless Gate", 1977

Discourse

Madurai, India, 1973

Bodhnath, Nepal, 1976

Krishna guard, 1981

Poona 1981

Poona 1988

Beedie time

Namaste

Energy darshan

Celebration in Buddha Hall

Ashram canteen, featuring Deeksha

Mala Shop workers

Sannyasin kids: Siddhartha (l.) & Deepa

-17-

And all the while, Osho was delivering. Morning after morning, he came out to give one marvel of a discourse after the other. While for the time being he continued to give the Hindi discourses in Chuang Tzu Auditorium, he had started in March 1977 to give the English discourses in the newly constructed Buddha Hall, so that the growing number of seekers could be accommodated.

Initially, it hadn't been much of a hall. When I first came to Poona, it had been merely a large, oval concrete slab, the central part of which was covered by a roof of corrugated tin of a more temporary character, and it was open on the sides. The wooden posts holding up the roof were simple, unfinished and crooked. The ceiling was covered with saris that were stretched out side by side so that you wouldn't be able to see the corrugated tin when inside the hall. There was a simple cloth screen, maybe seven feet tall, behind Osho's podium at the center of the north side of the hall. Only a couple of years later did the hall get a larger and more permanent roof consisting of corrugated asbestos sheets, held up by square wooden posts and proper horizontal supporting beams, all painted white.

If you wanted to sit as close to Osho as was possible under the circumstances, you took your place in the discourse line just after seven in the morning, which was when the Ashram opened its gates. And even then you were not at the beginning of the queue. The first places had been taken by some odd pieces of clothing belonging to people doing Dynamic, that traditionally had started at six. Those people joined the line sometime later, with bright eyes and full of energy. There was a troop of expert cleaners going for it now inside Buddha Hall to get the place shipshape, and they were moving their mops in a rhythmic dance, often to some hot rock music. You still had the time to go off to Vrindavan for a quick cup of coffee, before people were let in at seven thirty.

At the entrance, you were greeted by a sign, "Shoes and Minds are to be left at the Gate", next to which would generally be a rather unruly pile of shoes and sandals, until in later years a top- of-the-line shoe check was built. Once inside the hall, there was often a rather undignified rush for the best seats. The first ten rows or so were already taken by the cushions of the people who had reserved seats, and it was pretty much predetermined where those people would sit. And for those lucky ones there was no hurry to get to discourse, it was sufficient to show up just a few minutes before eight. For the rest of the hall, it was first come, first served. With a bit of luck you got a decent seat, hopefully behind a person that was not too tall, and next to people who were "good sitters" and had a friendly energy.

So, there you were now, and you were in for a lot of sitting, two hours at the least, on a hard cement floor, and you were faced with the eternal meditators' problem of what to do with those goddamn legs. Those New Age couch potato contraptions with back rests had not yet been invented, and that may have been for the better since I don't think they are very conductive to staying alert. They may be comfortable, but that's beside the point at an occasion like this. For my first year or two in Poona I was biding my time on a folded-up *lunghi*, and when I eventually graduated to a foam cushion and from there on to a super de luxe model made of coconut fibers it felt like a seat in paradise.

And that was Buddha Hall; the situation in Chuang Tzu Auditorium was much more grim. Since the place was often packed to the max, almost like a can of sardines, it was not permitted to bring in anything that you could sit on. Often we were almost literally breathing down the neck of the person in front of us, and on chilly winter mornings the terracotta floor was freezing cold. To avoid getting hemorrhoids or other physical ailments, which quite a few people did through this exercise, seasoned discourse goers would pad the seat of their pants with a *lunghi* or a small towel as a preventive measure, or to at least take the edge off the worst of the discomfort.

Well, in the end it didn't really matter once Osho filled the hall with his presence, and, if anything, this broke my body in pretty well to being able to sit motionlessly on the floor over long periods of time. This was certainly an asset, as that was the worst place imaginable to spend your time fidgeting and squirming around. I may have learned the hard way, but in this case I'd say that the end justifies the means. Fine, let Osho kick back in his La-Z-Boy, that was his privilege. But we were there to wake up, which is no cheap affair, and not for sissies. And if you had the guts, you rose to the occasion and paid whatever price there was to pay.

The outer form of the discourses followed a very simple and very strict routine, any deviations from which were so rare that they were practically nonexistent. It started with the pre-discourse ritual. Maybe ten minutes before eight, two berobed swamis would bring in Osho's chair that was covered with a dust cloth, and with precise, carefully choreographed movements set the chair down so that it would be in the exact position where it needed to be. Then the dust cloth was removed, carefully folded and taken out. Following that, another swami brought in the microphone on its stand and, measuring the distance to the chair with the help of the width and length of his hands, set up the stand in such a way that the microphone was precisely where it needed to be for Osho. (I have never seen Osho touch the microphone, either intentionally or accidentally. It was always exactly in its right place.)

During that whole time, there was a pin-drop silence in the hall, from the time the first people were let in until Osho started speaking. The only exception was an announcement at about five to eight asking everybody to remain in the hall for the whole duration of the discourse ("... until the car has left the compound."), and please not to cough.

One of the cardinal sins at the Ashram was coughing during discourse. If your throat was in a condition where you might not be able to contain your cough during that time, it was advisable to listen to the discourse outside of the hall, or at least to come prepared, with a couple of Hall's menthol candies in your pocket. If you were even wiser, you freed those of their wrappers before the discourse started ... you'd never believe how much noise it could create if you try to do that while the discourse was in progress. I have sat next to people who had a whole row of four or five Hall's lined up in front of them, all neatly placed on their opened wrappers, ready to be popped whenever the need should arise.

Now, when that no-coughing-announcement was made, you knew that this was your last chance for a final throat-clearing effort that, hopefully, would be good enough for the next hour and a half. And there were times when seemingly everybody else had the same idea, and for the next minute or so being in Buddha Hall was reminiscent of being in a TB ward.

Before we continue, a word about Osho's cars, a subject that to many people has been of more importance than anything else he's said or done ... or been. Originally, it had been a beige Chevrolet Impala, one of those big, gas-guzzling dinosaurs, in which he was driven every morning from Lao Tzu House to Buddha Hall, a distance that might have taken him about two or three minutes to walk. Already that fact drew many comments ... what kind of a guru was that?

In 1978, Osho upped the ante and told Laxmi to go and purchase the most expensive car that she could find, which turned out to be a late-model, yellow Mercedes. He said that it would help her to obtain loans at the bank (which reportedly it did), and besides, he had found out that in America, a Chevrolet is a plumber's car, and he didn't want to be driven around in something like *that*.

It was in December 1979 that we got our first Rolls-Royce, and its plain white color did nothing to diminish the overall impression that this was one very expensive set of wheels. For India, this was nothing short of sensational. It didn't take long before Osho also became known as the "Rolls-Royce Guru", besides "Sex Guru", "Rich Man's Guru" and several other titles. When he showed up at Buddha Hall in the Rolls for the first time on his birthday, there was a ripple of laughter that went from one end of the hall to the other. And if we thought we'd seen everything, we were wrong. Just wait a few more years ...

Back to Buddha Hall, time for discourse. At eight o' clock, a crunch of gravel could be heard, the car with Osho inside drove up, he got out and entered the hall, his hands raised in the traditional Indian "namaste" greeting. Dressed in a plain white robe and moving as lightly and gracefully as a falling feather, he walked up onto the podium, stopped in front of his chair, and, turning slowly from his right to his left, extended his namaste to everyone in the hall, before sitting down. To me, this has always been a moment of incomparable dignity and grace, where I was just holding my breath in awe. And even then, when I'd see him enter the hall, there had always been a subtle feeling of, "Wow! He came out one more time ...", as if something in me had been trying to tell me that someday that would not be the case anymore. Then, it had seemed that those days with Osho would go on forever ...

If it was a "sutra day", it was now Teertha's turn to read them out (or Taru's to sing them, if it was a Hindi discourse); if it was a "question day", Osho would bring his head just a tad forward towards the microphone and start with, "The first question", and the discourse was on.

At the end, he would close with, "Enough for today" (or, "Aj itna hee", at the end of a Hindi discourse), get up, namaste, and get into the car. The car would then slowly drive around Buddha Hall, the three quarters of the route that were needed to complete a full circle, proceeding counterclockwise, and then head back home to Lao Tzu House. (Years later, on the Ranch, he'd be following the same procedure - circling Rajneesh Mandir in a counterclockwise direction, and there, as in Poona, his podium would be in the center of the northern part of the hall, so that he would be speaking from that direction. Coincidence or esoteric design?)

As far as the actual discourse went, anybody who has ever been there or seen one on video or read any of Osho's books knows that the sky was the limit as to what he'd be able to pull out of his hat (metaphorically speaking, since during those days he didn't wear one, except for occasional photo sessions). But the format, the way he came in, greeted us, and left, was always exactly the same, down to the smallest, minute movement. If there was ever the slightest change, that was a minor sensation.

I want to relate a small incident to you, as an example. In Buddha Hall, as well as in Chuang Tzu Auditorium, there was a clock maybe twenty or thirty feet away from the podium and facing it, so that Osho could see what time it was in order to time his discourse. It happened during a Hindi discourse, that, what must have been towards the end, I saw Osho giving a short glance towards that clock. A couple of minutes later, another glance, and then he stopped, turned to Teertha who was sitting at his customary place right in the center of the first row, and asked (in English), "Teertha, what is the time?", and then adding something about the clock that had stopped. Teertha looked at his wristwatch and told Osho the time, who then continued with the Hindi discourse, to conclude it a few minutes later. This small, out-of-the-order incident just blew everybody's mind, and for the rest of the day the Ashram was totally a-buzz with it.

***

-18-

Osho's discourses were laced with one ingredient that everybody loved, which was a sense of humor that was nothing short of divine. It was never that his discourses ever felt dry or theoretical. They were so alive and sparkling that just that would have been enough. Still, right in the middle of talking about some spiritual theme he'd all the sudden change gears and launch a few well-placed one-liners that had everybody cracking up and gasping for air, that got you out of the deepest meditation right back into the here and now of Buddha Hall, or he'd relate one of his hilariously funny anecdotes that he often made up right on the spot.

Besides being very capable of improvising and looking at the funny side of just about any matter, he also came to discourse well prepared. After taking his seat, Laxmi or Vivek, who had entered the hall behind him, would come up to the podium to hand him a small clipboard. This held a few small scraps of paper, containing the day's sutras or questions, as well as a number of jokes. Usually, he used those to illustrate a subject he was speaking on, and, at the appropriate point during the discourse, introduced the joke with the line, "I have heard ... ". About this he was very particular, because, as he said, he could not guarantee that it was actually the truth.

And no joke was too juicy or outrageous not to be shared by him. Whether they were about minorities or contained four-letter words, Osho dished them up, with a relish. He was very well aware of any linguistic taboos that might exist, and he played with just about all of them. He did not even shy back from taking a few cracks at the most evil word in the English language, a word that is so bad that in puritan America it is widely referred to only as the "f-word". Well, I take it by now y'all know which word we're talking about. "There are no dirty words, only dirty minds," as he once put the whole subject into the right perspective. So, on occasion, he either came up with gems like, "I like to call a spade a spade, and sometimes a fucking spade", or he read out a joke that contained the magic word.

Most of us loved him even more for that, but there were a few in the audience that did have a bit of a problem with it. The real problem, though, is how the mind is conditioned, and how deep that can go I'd see years later when I was living in the States. There was one incident when, while just chatting with someone at work, I dropped the word, and, in that instant, I saw something like a jolt go through the whole body of that poor guy. There were also a couple of books that I'd signed out from the local public library (just regular bestselling novels, by no means anything pornographic), where somebody had, throughout the books, carefully whited out every f-word in the text. (And, lastly, the dictionary I am using these days, "The New Merriam-Webster", with "today's essential vocabulary", has 60,000 entries, but guess which word is not among them.)

To set the matter straight, in April 1980 Osho pulled off a beauty that was to enter the akashic records as the famous "Fuck Discourse". During the discourses on Buddha's Dhammapada, somebody had sent in a question in which he expressed shock about Osho's use of the word "fuck". In his response, Osho quoted a small text that somebody had written on the grammatical and other uses of the word "fuck" in the English language.

What went on while he read out this text to us is almost beyond description. The whole of Buddha Hall went totally bananas. We were all roaring with laughter, rolling on the floor, our bellies were aching and tears of laughter were streaming down our faces. We barely had enough time to catch our breath before Osho fired off yet another meticulously timed salvo, and then again, and again, and again. By the time he came to a conclusion with his customary "enough for today", I was lying there on the floor of Buddha Hall, feeling as if a freight train had run over me, just asking myself in disbelief, "What the fuck was *that*?"

It was not only that it had been *him* who'd done it, or the subject matter, but also the absolutely light, sincere and innocent manner in which he had delivered the whole thing. To me, this was another prime example of how totally in charge of the situation he was, how he pushed every button he could find, how he just played with the energy, in a truly masterful fashion.

Yet, I have never seen Osho laugh, about any of the jokes he told or otherwise, except for maybe a chuckle during *darshan*. He always totally kept his cool. But it was quite apparent that he very much enjoyed it when he had us cracking up all over the place, when he, like after that discourse, got up, namasted and left the hall with one of his wonderful, radiant smiles on his face.

(Note: For the full text of the "Fuck Discourse", see Appendix "F" at the end of this tale.)

***

-19-

Wherever ignorance was at work, Osho shed his light on it. One of his favorite subjects was the politicians. He mercilessly exposed what they were truly motivated by, or they became the butt end of his jokes. The Indian prime minister at the time, Morarji Desai, was a conservative Hindu who had publicly spoken about his practice of drinking his own urine, which actually is a bona fide ayurvedic method to cleanse one's body, and Osho never missed a chance of poking some fun at this. On another occasion, he remarked that in the new commune there was going to be a sign at the entrance, "Dogs and politicians not allowed". The next day, he took it back, saying that it was unfair towards the dogs. (Indira Gandhi supposedly liked and respected Osho, but never went very much public about this, and Osho left her pretty much alone.)

Of course, these exploits had their consequences. The political caste made it as difficult as possible for the Ashram to carry out Osho's work. The widespread rumor was that the Ashram had to grease many palms and paid large sums of *baksheesh* to be able to continue, otherwise the authorities would have just shut the place down, and they'd have found reasons enough. One person who had summed it up quite nicely was Poona's Chief of Police, who reportedly had said, "This man (Osho) is so dangerous that he should be banned not only from Poona and India, but from the whole planet." Quite a compliment, actually, to be coming from a cop, and in its substance not one bit off the mark.

What was of particular embarrassment for many Indians, not only the politicians, was the extensive press coverage of the Ashram by the foreign media and their focus on sex and violence. No, the Indian government did "not look favorably at the activities of the Ashram", which resulted in foreign journalists, TV- and film crews being denied permission to cover the Ashram. Of course, they were inventive and found ways around and once they arrived, we had a well-staffed press office to give them just what they wanted. A German film company even went as far as shooting a full-length feature film there, "Ashram in Poona", that also showed explicit scenes from encounter-type groups, and that turned out to be a big hit in German cinemas.

In another matter it once again was the corruption of the Indian political system that came to our assistance. Unless you were as lucky as to come from a country within the British Commonwealth (then), all foreigners needed a visa for India, which was initially easy enough to obtain, but it got a bit sticky once you had been there for half a year and wanted to stay on any longer. Help did come along, in the form of a fat little Indian guy named Moses who was frequently seen hanging out around the Ashram, and who was known by virtually everybody. "Visa? No problem!" He appeared to be so well connected that he could fix just about any visa situation, provided you could cough up the necessary dough. It was also rumored that on occasion he liked to take a cute ma to bed as compensation for his services. And towards the end of Poona I, he even took sannyas!

There was another guy who took the law into his own hands to express his hatred towards Osho, a Hindu fundamentalist named Vilas Tupe. On May 22, 1980, during a Hindi discourse in Buddha Hall, there was all of a sudden a commotion in the rear of the hall. I turned around, just in time to see a man who had stood up and was shouting something at Osho, and, judging by the tone of his voice, those were no pleasantries at all. Before anybody could react, he pulled out a large knife and threw that towards Osho. Lucky enough, the throw was short and the knife landed a few feet from the podium.

He was quickly apprehended by some sannyasins, taken out of the hall and handed over to the police (who, believe it or not, had been tipped off, and several of them were present in the hall, in plain clothes!!), before Osho continued with his discourse, seemingly unruffled. But, in a fine display of the corrupted Indian legal system, the case against Tupe was dropped soon afterwards and he was released. (Personally, I wouldn't want to live with that kind of a karma, in jail or not...)

A consequence of this incident was a beefed up security at the Ashram, and, within a few days, everybody going to discourse had to pass through a walk-thru metal detector, and after that get frisked. Before that, the only "check" we had to go through had been the "sniffers". On the way into Buddha Hall, there was a line of (usually very pretty) mas, facing each other in pairs. You had to pass through a pair, and, while doing so, briefly stop while they were doing a deep breath inhalation. Anybody with a strong odor of tobacco smoke, perfume, soap etc. was asked to sit in the back of the hall, far away from Osho, who was very allergic against strong odors. Extreme cases were asked to remain outside. I presume that this system was also used to weed out people with bad vibes, but on that day it had failed.

***

-20-

My career as a handyman came to an abrupt end during the next monsoon, in the summer of 1980, when I got the job to go up onto a roof to make some repairs there. An hour or so earlier it had rained, the tiles were more slippery than I thought them to be, and before I was really up on that roof I was sliding down again. I fell about ten feet to the ground and landed with my right heel first on a very hard and unyielding cement surface, which put a good crack into my heel bone. Ouch, that hurt! I got a nice cast on my foot and was seen hobbling around on crutches for the next seven weeks. Some people even called me "peg leg"!

This may all sound quite dramatic, but I was beautifully taken care of by the commune. After a week in the Ashram ward I went back to work, as a receptionist for the group facilities at the Music House, another property the Ashram had rented nearby. There wasn't really much to do, I was just sitting there in that chair all day, watching who was coming in, and smoking a lot of beedies. Friends would drop by for a chat, and, now that I couldn't run away any more, beautiful mas would come and sit on my lap.

Being involved in a situation like this helped the healing process more than anything else. And it also was a great teaching, in many ways. Since I was on crutches, I had to ask for help a lot of times (like getting my lunch tray), and some kind soul (actually, it was one of the group leaders) gave me the extremely valuable piece of advice, "Watch how you ask - don't whine, and don't demand."

After the cast came off, I slowly and very painfully had to learn how to walk again, and it took a lot of effort to eventually let go of my crutches. During that whole time I had to sit in the "cripple section" during discourse, which consisted of a few chairs way in the back of Buddha Hall. On the day when I was finally able to sit on the floor again (and much closer to the podium), it was no other than Osho who, in the course of the discourse, said, "I am going to take all your crutches away!" as a warning of what was yet to come.

***

-21-

The Music House, "Somji Estate" by its proper name, consisted of a large building on a sizable piece of property. In addition to the group rooms, the Ashram operated a restaurant in the house called "Somji Kitchen" that served Indian-style meals. In recent months, most of the new food passes the Ashram had issued were only good for here, because conditions at Mariam Canteen had been getting too crowded. Also on the premises were maybe twenty bamboo huts in which sannyasins were living.

Mainly to prevent Indians from snooping around that had nothing to do here, there was a guard on duty that was furnished by the group department. This seemed to be quite an easy job. Most of the time, the guard was just lounging around in his hut, smoking beedies and chatting with the ladies.

To the extent that I was able to walk again, I was reintegrated into the active work process. I helped to set up group rooms, did a bit of cleaning and also started to give breaks to our guard. Now, this was an activity just to my liking. Not so long afterwards one of the two guards who covered that position was going back to the West, and the job was becoming vacant. I inquired discreetly through my coordinator whether it would be possible for me to continue in that line of work, and I got a positive answer.

In a further development, the guards department of the Ashram then took over the responsibility for security at the Music House. I was taken over along with the inventory, so to speak, and so it happened that I became a guard, a job that came with considerable social prestige and an impressively looking, maroon uniform that was modeled after the outfits worn by Judokas. "Krishna Guards", we were called (and by coincidence Krishna was also the name of our coordinator), not to be confused with the "Samurai", the elite warriors guarding Lao Tzu House.

After a few weeks, I was transferred to a position in the Ashram itself, but first I had to go through an experience that went a bit further than just chasing a couple of babas off the grounds, and that was a valid reminder that there were also some responsibilities that came with my job. One day while I was on duty, a few sannyasins brought an Indian thief to me that they had caught on the premises. Hmm, what to do with him? I sent somebody down to the Ashram for help while I was trying to hold on to the poor guy, with one of his arms in a restraining hold behind his back. Around us a whole group of onlookers had gathered, sannyasins as well as Indians, and for them this was some real live action.

So there we were, the robber and the cop, along with our audience. He was whining and bitching and squirming and was anything but pleasant company. The sun was beating down, it seemed to be getting hotter by the minute, and both of us were sweating so much that a couple of times he almost slipped out of my grip. Finally, after what had felt like an eternity, but in reality was only about 20 minutes, another guard came from the Ashram with a rickshaw and took him away. (What we actually did with cases like that was that we gave them a good spanking before turning them loose - if we'd hand them over to the police, nothing would happen.) The incident left me quite drained and shaken up inside, and it took me a few hours to get rid of the bad vibes I'd taken on from the guy.

***

-22-

My new position at the Ashram was that of the "rounder", which was actually not a fixed position, as the name implies. Besides giving breaks to the other positions at certain times, my main duty while on evening or night shift was to go on rounds throughout the Ashram (except for Lao Tzu House and the grounds around it). I had to check that everything was as it was supposed to be. Doors had to be locked, lights and fans had to be switched off, and that this was done was the responsibility of the people working there during the day. Furthermore, I had to keep my eyes peeled for anything that might constitute a safety- or security hazard.

The Ashram as it was then was a labyrinth of work- and living spaces. Since the Indian authorities had been stalling to give us any new building permits, we had done a lot of illegal building, some of it in a more permanent form, some of it more improvised. If any small bit of space could be utilized in some way, then it was done. Especially on the roofs of the buildings my rounds took me along some pretty adventurous routes, and the nighttime energy at the Ashram added a very extraordinary flavor to that.

When I was on morning or afternoon shift, I spent a good part of my time running errands for Krishna, during the course of which I also had the opportunity to find out what the rounders of the previous night had detected. In those cases I had to go to the respective department coordinators to kindly remind them that they had left the door of their work space unlocked, or a fan had been left switched on, and to please be more aware in the future (and it was very advisable not to come across as too German on those occasions, jawohl?).

There was also a cute small job I had to do during the morning shift at twenty past six, which was when the "hoo"-phase of Dynamic was starting. I had to position myself at the rear edge of Buddha Hall and watch that none of the meditators (who were then jumping up and down, shouting the Sufi mantra "hoo, hoo", and many of them were blindfolded) were falling over the edge of the hall. (This turned out to be very beneficial for my karma - there is hardly anything that brings more karmic merits than when you save a soul that is trying to meditate. I can still feel the effects today!)

When I was on morning shift, this also meant that I could not go to discourse. Still, I got a very decent deal. During that time, I was positioned at the gate of the book bindery, halfway between the eastern end of Buddha Hall and the entrance to Lao Tzu. This was right along the route Osho's car took to and from discourse, and that way I got an extra and personal namaste from my master.

Those were the best times I'd ever had in Poona. I was just flying with my work, and totally loved it. The rounders of the different shifts were in an undeclared competition for who would score the most points, whose list of findings that we placed on Krishna's desk at the end of our shift was the longest. Before long, I was feared for my thoroughness and mercilessness, and I also brought in several trophies for Krishna. Once it was an electronic calculator (an expensive item in India at the time) that I'd taken from an office where I found the sliding customer service window unlocked, another time it was a bottle of Kingfisher Lager from a beer cooler at the Ashram bar that had been left open. (Those were, of course, returned the next morning.) Admittedly, I went a bit overboard a couple of times when I found a way into Vrindavan, and the cookies I scored on those occasions did not go on Krishna's desk, but were shared among my fellow guards.

There was no doubt in my mind, or heart, that I was absolutely where I wanted to be, and that I was doing what I wanted to do. I had my place in the commune, I wasn't going anywhere. I was at home. Still, we all knew that it was not going to last forever.

***

-23-

By early 1981, the Ashram was booming like never before. There were at least two or three times as many people here than when I had first come, and the place was literally starting to burst at its seams. I've met people who back then had the feeling of having arrived too late. Most everybody knew that *something* was going to happen. Osho continued to make frequent remarks about that "new commune", and when Teertha leaked out one day that we were "never going to believe the changes that were going to happen this year", that only added more fuel to the fire. There were times when the Ashram seemed to be overflowing with gossip and rumors, and as a countermeasure, word came down from the Ashram management that it was strictly forbidden to spread any rumors. Fat chance!

Then Osho went into silence. At first it did not even appear to be that. On March 10, he had given the last discourse of the series, "The Goose Is Out". The next morning he did not come out - supposedly his body was not well - nor were there discourses during the weeks that followed. Nobody really knew what was going on. Then, on April 10, he sent a message through Laxmi that he would from now on speak only through the language of silence, and that this would be the ultimate phase of his work.

It was also announced that, starting on May 1, Osho would be giving silent satsangs. (By definition, satsang means to be in the presence of an awakened being. From Sanskrit "sat", meaning truth, being, and "sangha", meaning community.) This got the Ashram really humming. Buddha Hall was completely remodeled, a new podium was built that was a bit higher than the old one, and we even raised the elevation of the driveway behind Buddha Hall by about two feet, so that Osho would be able to leave his car and get onto his stage without having to climb any steps. From what I heard it was his back pains that were the most serious of his health problems, so we were making it as easy and comfortable for him as possible to come out and sit with us.

Still, although the results of our building activities had a certain solidity to them, were quite tangible and appeared rather permanent, there was a quality of uncertainty in the air, of impending change, many of us did feel deep inside that we were heading for the *Grand Finale*. What gave some credibility to this were the traveling activities of Sheela, Laxmi's assistant, who had been to the States several times in the past weeks. Also, in a rather hushed-up move, a group of about a dozen crack carpenters and handymen were sent to renovate the "Castle", as the building housing the Chidvilas Rajneesh Meditation Center in Montclair, New Jersey, was called. Chidvilas had been developed into the largest sannyasin media center in the western world and was run by Jayananda, Sheela's second husband, who also happened to be an investment banker by trade.

The May satsangs to me were the true climax of my Poona days, perhaps of my whole time as a sannyasin. They just rolled over me, and left me feeling incredibly high. What made them even more intense and added a very unique flavor to them, almost like a few grains of salt, was that Osho was going to leave us. This was never officially announced, but many of us just knew.

Every morning, he came out and sat with us, and it was very obvious that his body was not well. Once, he needed three attempts until he was able to get up from his chair that had been designed especially for him. Between periods of silence, there were readings of Kahlil Gibran's "Prophet", and the Ashram musicians, led by Yashu, Chaitanya Hari and Govinddas, played some of their best music ever. When I listen to some of those tunes today, they still invoke the magic of those days for me.

On June 1, during the morning hours, Lao Tzu gate opened, and the white Rolls-Royce with Osho inside was slowly driven towards the main gate. Whoever happened to be there had the opportunity for a last namaste. My old friend Kirti who was on guard duty at the gate rolled it open, the Rolls went past, and then it was gone. In Bombay, Osho and a few close disciples boarded a Pan Am jet and left, bound for New York, and from there on to the Castle.

***

-24-

So, there we were. The master had flown the coop. Within a few days, it was becoming very clear what was going on, the dice were cast. The Ashram was closing down, and we were going to have our "new commune" in far-away America. Although there had been plenty of rumors to that effect, this came as a bit of a surprise to many of us. And a lot of us were quite thrilled, since we had become somewhat weary of living in India. While there were some that were feeling lost, disoriented or even devastated, others were in good spirits and immediately started to scheme and plan how they were going to catch up with Osho.

The big question for anybody committed to being in the commune became, "How am I going to get there?" The official line from the Ashram was, "Go back to where you came from and wait, we'll call you." However, we knew it wasn't going to be the same for everybody, and the new commune certainly wasn't a place where you could just go to – it was by invitation only.

Meanwhile, word came over from New Jersey that Osho was fine there, that he was going out on occasional cruises in his Rolls and that he was playing frisbee on the lawn in front of the Castle, wearing an "I love NY" T-shirt and shorts (the latter, I must add, did not prove to be factually correct).

For the time being, though, we had to concentrate on the business at hand; we couldn't just pack up and leave in a day or two. Demolition crews were working 24 hours a day to take down all the structures we had built illegaly. Buddha Hall was torn down, leaving only a bare, oval concrete slab. Other crews were working around the clock to pack tens of thousands of Osho's books and his whole library into wooden crates to be shipped to the US. On my late-night rounds through the Ashram, I'd see them taking breaks, standing in circles and giving neck- and back-massages to each other. There was a big sale going on of Ashram property like sound- or electronic equipment, as well as all kinds of stuff from individual sannyasins that were leaving. Particularly at night the Ashram emanated an almost eerie feeling, which was accentuated by the monsoon rains and by the ensuing dampness.

Being sannyasins, we did it with our customary gusto. One of the big movies during the seventies had been "The Last Tango in Paris", starring Marlon Brando. In a take-off on the title, our silk screen-printing department created T-shirts with "The Last Mango in Poona" printed on them, which were a big hit with the sannyasins celebrating their departure. When Mariam Canteen closed to merge with Vrindavan, we had a "last supper" there, by candlelight, with wine and on real tablecloths.

The Indian business community was less excited, though, which was expressed in a headline of the *Poona Herald* reading, "A Recession Named Rajneesh". After all, we had spent *lakhs* and *lakhs* of rupees in Poona, and at least moneywise we were certainly going to be missed.

And just about as little excited was an unfortunate swami that I met, who, a couple of months before, had been out of the loop of what was coming down and had invested all his money in bamboo huts that he was going to rent out to sannyasins. He was not going to be sitting at the feet of the master now, while the rupees were rolling in by themselves. The only thing he got back was the scrap value.

Many of us who had been here for a long time were going to have a problem just getting out of India, since our visas had expired long ago. I hadn't had a valid visa for way over a year, but I was lucky. The Ashram made a deal with the Indian immigration authorities for long-term workers and ashramites, and I got my exit stamp, no questions asked.

Still, I didn't really have any place I wanted to go back to. I had no connections to any Osho center or sannyasin community in the West, nor did my native Germany appear like a very attractive place to live, even for a limited time, until I'd get "called", whenever that might be. So Devika, my American girlfriend and I decided to stay together and, via Germany, go on to the US to see what we could do there.

***

PART III:
THE RANCH

-25-

Devika and I left Poona in mid-August and, via Germany, went on to the States in early October. We were staying at her parents' place in San Diego and were just checking out the local sannyasin scene when she was contacted by Geetam, an Osho center in southern California, whether she would like to come to live and work there as a resident. And yes, I lucked out and could come, too. So, in late October we left for the desert, and, looking back, it appeared to have been an incredibly smooth ride.

Geetam was located about 30 miles as the crow flies northeast of San Bernardino, way out in the countryside near the small town of Lucerne Valley, on the edge of the Mojave desert. What made it special was that when the Ashram in Poona closed down, the group department was moved there. All the hot-shot therapists and body workers were there, plus between 40 and 50 residents to run the place, and in addition to that the (paying) participants in the groups and other programs.

Originally it had been a rather laid-back sannyasin center, complete with hot tub and swimming pool, but that had changed quite drastically with the advent of the group department. Just the sheer amount of people needing a place to stay stretched the capacity of the place to the limit, so many of us were living in tents. (I have to add that these were quite comfortable – they were put up on wooden platforms, hooked up to electricity and equipped with kerosene heaters that were needed in the cold desert nights.)

I got a job in the maintenance department, fixing all kinds of things. The work went fine, the hours were agreeable, the food was excellent and every evening at five we would get together at "happy hour" for a glass of beer or wine to unwind. Still, the energy of the place was very intense.

Among sannyasins there had always been a rather relaxed attitude regarding sexual promiscuity, and here it was even more relaxed. I had come there pretty much as a part of a one-on-one couple, but it didn't take long before we both joined the Big Party that was going on. This added an enormous amount of juice to whatever other button-pushing was going on during the work. We went through incredible stuff regarding jealousy, possessiveness and everything else connected with relationships.

I remember once, after a full moon night, I came to work in the morning, took a good look at a couple of my co-workers, and we realized that we'd all been hit pretty hard the previous night. So, under the pretense to fix something somewhere, we took off into the desert, sat down in a shady spot, chain-smoked Camels and did a lot of sharing. Like before, in Poona, and later on the Ranch, it was that love and understanding and support that enabled us to face whatever was coming up through the work and otherwise. That was one of the main reasons we were here for - how can you get to know the deeper realms of your being when you don't know what kind of stuff is hidden just beneath the surface?

Although the Ranch was off some 800 miles to the north, we all felt very close to what was happening there … and to Osho. The management at Geetam was in regular phone contact with "The Land", as we called it, and occasionaly somebody would go up there on some business. Upon that person's return, we'd have a "family meeting", where we would get a first-hand account: Osho stories, gossip on how our friends were doing that were already there, and any kind of other information - we'd sit there with glowing eyes and soak it up like a sponge.

It became apparent that for most of us Geetam would be a jumping board to get to the new commune. Osho wanted to have as many people there as possible, so the priority was to set up as much housing as was technically feasible. In those first months we bought dozens of prefabricated houses, over-length, double-width "trailers". They were rolled in, sited and connected to electricity and water. Each had eight bedrooms, two bathrooms, living room and kitchen, and could be occupied immediately. And at Geetam we'd know when another trailer or two were ready, because that was when the word would come down from the Ranch for a few lucky ones to pack their bags and come on up.

For Devika and me the time came in February 1982. The family meeting where the announcement was made turned into the usual farewell party, with lots of hugs and smiles and tears. Two days later, the two of us and another swami put our few belongings into an old pick-up truck and headed north.

***

-26-

At first glance, "The Land" appeared to be anything but hospitable. When we came to the edge of the property in the waning daylight, greeted by a "Rancho Rajneesh" sign by the roadside, we caught a glimpse of seemingly endless hills that were dotted with juniper trees and were gently sloping down towards the John Day River that was bordering the property in the east. We seemed to be in the middle of nowhere. There was a bit of snow on the ground, and a cold drizzle was coming down.

By the time we made it down the winding and unpaved road to the actual Ranch, it was dark. Since it was already past dinner time, most of the people there were off to their homes and the place appeared rather quiet and deserted. And at Mahakashyap Reception, a sign on the wall informed us that "If it weren't so hard, it would be too easy". Still, we were expected. There were some sandwiches ready for us, and we were driven to our trailer, a few miles further down a muddy road and then steeply up a hill. We were too tired to register very much more.

When we looked out of our bedroom window the next morning we were awed by the view. We were high up on the slope of a hill, overlooking a wide valley with a small creek at the bottom. There were a couple of other trailers in the vicinity, a few hundred yards away. And way down, about a mile away, on the lower parts of the opposing hillside, was Magdalena Cafeteria.

As it turned out, due to the local zoning laws we were not permitted to build just anywhere. The land was classified for agricultural use, which meant that only a certain number of buildings could be put up in a given sector of land.

The original ranch buildings (now that area was called Jesus Grove) were at the confluence of two creeks that, a few miles onwards, emptied into the John Day River (or, rather, Radha River, as we had renamed it). There wasn't an awful lot of flat land. The valleys that the creeks ran in were rather narrow, at the most maybe half a mile wide. And the valleys were surrounded by hills, and those by even more hills, all with small, sometimes canyon - like dry valleys between them, and covered with sparse grass, sagebrush and a few juniper trees.

Still, the land certainly had its own, stark beauty, that was accentuated in places by imposing and bizarre rock formations that some of the hills were adorned with. Yes, this was Western country, and even John Wayne himself starred in a movie, "Rooster Cogburn", that was shot in the area years ago.

As a consequence, you had to cover quite a distance to move around the commune which, particularly in the early days, took some effort. The existing roads were not paved, and huge clouds of dust were trailing behind moving cars. During wet weather, things were quite muddy. In fact, the mud, from which the original name of the Ranch, "The Big Muddy", had been derived, seemed to be everywhere. And every building had an entrance room where we would take off our shoes that was aptly called the "mud room".

A few years later, we'd have the most extensive public transport system in the state of Oregon ("Rajneesh Buddhafield Transport"), but initially all we had was an old school bus that would pick people up in the morning for breakfast, do a run at lunch time and take a round or two after dinner to bring everybody home. Beyond that, during the day it was quite easy to hitch a ride with any of the trucks, pick-ups or other vehicles that we had and that were necessary to do the work. However, if you got stuck somewhere at night, in a lot of cases it meant that you had to walk home, which could take up to an hour. No rickshaws here, baba!

It wasn't much of a problem though to make it down to Maggie's Cafe for breakfast (just slide down that muddy hill, and then plod back up again a bit on the other side). And this was the place where everybody met everybody else. What a blast to see old friends again that I hadn't seen since Poona! So many hugs and smiling faces, and then the stories we all had to tell ... man, here I was, home once more.

Among the 300 to 350 people here there were many I had never seen before, and everybody looked quite different than back in India. Gone were the robes and sandals and the loose, flowing dresses. They had been replaced by western, rather unisex clothing of the rugged outdoor type with heavy boots, and some people were sporting cowboy hats. Most of the swamis had cut their long hair (as I had myself upon leaving Poona), and some had even shaved off their beards. We'd undergone a transition, from hippie to cowboy. But everybody was healthy and happy and full of zest. These were still the pioneer days, and life had a beautiful quality of simplicity, earthiness and innocence to it.

And of course, Osho was here. His trailer was tucked away in a scenic side valley called Lao Tzu Grove (or, in Ranch jargon, "B-Site"). His health had improved visibly, and he was still in silence.

Every day at 2 pm he would go out for a ride in a shiny Rolls-Royce. This was when we all lined up by the side of the road to greet him with a namaste. He'd slow down, raise one of his hands in greeting and look at each one of us in passing by … and then disappear in a cloud of dust.

Compared to the juice he had doled out in Poona, these appeared to be rather homeopathic doses. Still, depending on how open you were and what you needed, these encounters could be quite intense … a *darshan* on the road. We all felt incredibly blessed to be able to be here with him. That was all that really mattered. And certainly, if it weren't for him, none of us would be here.

***

-27-

There was an enormous amount of work waiting for us. We wanted to bring in many more people to live here permanently, and we wanted to make it possible for anybody who wished to do so to come and participate in groups, workshops and educational programs, and to participate in commune life on a temporary basis. Osho's vision had a very practical side to it, and this was going to be the main place where it was going to happen. For this, a city was needed, complete with buildings and the necessary infrastructure.

As far as our legal situation at the time was concerned, though, all we could strive for was to be an "agricultural commune". And given the potential of the land and our own aspirations, that did have its limitations. We already had many more people here than were needed for an "agricultural commune", and we were starting to bend the rules a little. Neighbors and officials in governmental institutions had started to become suspicious of us almost immediately, and that was not only because we wore red clothes and had those funny necklaces around our neck, because there was this Indian guru amongst us that was driving around in a fat Rolls- Royce or because we seemed to have an almost unlimited amount of money at our disposal. ("Jesus saves, Moses invests, Bhagwan spends", as one of the Ranch bumper stickers read.) There was something in us that made us decidedly different from the rest of the Oregonians, and I can't blame them when they must have asked themselves, "Now, what are *those* guys gonna be up to?"

For now, we tried to keep up a certain front as much as possible, and to explore avenues of procedure that we could follow and still build our city, lawfully. For starters, in early 1982 we incorporated part of the property as the City of Rajneeshpuram.

I started to work in Chuang Tzu, the construction department, and joined a crew that was finishing off the interior of Zarathustra, a large sheet metal building that was supposedly for the storage of agricultural produce, but was in reality housing hundreds of wooden crates containing Osho's books and library that had been shipped over from India. We hung drywall in the office part of the building, and put in doors and windows.

A week or two later, we moved down the road to Mahavira that was going to house the heavy equipment department, doing the same type of work. When that was done, we went on to Jesus Grove and built an extension to Sheela's trailer, and from there on to remodel one of the old ranch buildings to create a new home for Naropa, the publishing department.

We worked hard, but in a relaxed manner. We had a lot of fun with each other, and we also got our buttons pushed. Plenty. It was not only the work that accomplished that, we also treated one another generously. And sure enough, sometimes you ended up with a couple of jerks in your crew. But however hard it got, there was always somebody there to hug or to share with or a shoulder to cry on. There was an incredible and inexhaustible amount of love around the commune that was the perfect counterpart for any kind of hardship we might be going through, that made anything bearable.

Yes, we did take care of each other, and we were very good at it, in many different ways.

Our trailers were cleaned daily, and when we came home in the evenings our laundry was waiting for us on our beds, washed, dried and folded. At Pythagoras, we had a small clinic that was supplemented by a number of world-class body workers and chiropractors. Those were in very high demand as due to the hard physical work and a multitude of emotional strains a lot of necks and backs went out. One of the forms of "preventive care" was that every month during the full moon, announcements were made on the PA system at Maggie's to be extra careful on the road, on construction sites and elsewhere.

My favorite though, was the dentist. If you wanted, you could put on earphones and listen to soothing music while your teeth were being worked on. If it was getting a bit rough, there was a beautiful ma at your side to hold your hand, and when you opened your eyes, Osho was smiling down at you from a picture tacked to the ceiling. With all that, who'd need nitrous oxide?

The first major building that had been finished on the Ranch was the cafeteria, just in time for Osho's golden birthday celebration on December 11, 1981. And in my whole time there I have never experienced a day when we were not treated to three delicious meals a day.

Besides a sumptuous breakfast buffet, there was always a warm lunch and dinner, with piles of lettuce and sprouts, and additionally even brown rice and tofu for those of us who wanted to diet. (All in all, though, I guess the tendency was rather that people were gaining weight, and that not only in the form of muscle mass on ass-busting construction workers.) Once a week was "junk food day", with soy burgers and soy hot dogs, and about once a month we had the vegetarian version of a traditional Thanksgiving dinner, mock turkey with all the trimmings - stuffing, gravy, mashed potatoes, cranberries and pumpkin pie. Yum, that was absolutely dee-fucking-licious, time for pigging out!

The cuisine was strictly vegetarian (although certainly not vegan, nor was sugar or the like missing - it was left up to the individual what he or she wanted to eat). Osho has always given us a very free hand as to what we wanted to do, as long as we did something consciously, and not habitually, but about one thing he was very clear: in the communes around him there was to be no consumption of meat or meat products, including fish (but not excluding eggs or dairy products). His bottom line was that it is "simply ugly" to kill such highly evolved beings as animals for your food, when you can just as well get all the nourishment you need from vegetarian sources.

Over time, more and more of the produce came right from our own truck farm, and we also started to bake our own top-quality bread (there were enough Germans among us that knew about that one).

The only thing I might have to complain about was that at some point the generous choice of jams for breakfast was replaced with grape jelly, and grape jelly only, and grape jelly it was going to be until the end. God, I'm cured of that stuff for the rest of my life.

Our working day typically started at eight in the morning. At 1 pm we'd take an hour off for lunch, and then line up on the road for Osho's drive-by. There was a 20 minute break ("tea time" ... after all, we'd come from India) during the morning, and another one during the afternoon, that often went on for 30 minutes or more, with plenty of coffee, tea, fixings for peanut butter-jelly sandwiches and sometimes chocolate chip cookies. (What we had depended very much on what our "tea moms" were able to scrounge at Maggie's ... there were times we had regular feasts.)

Dinner was at seven. We'd hang out over a glass of beer and socialize a bit, but mostly we were too tired to feel like going for a lot of action. There wasn't really any place to go, anyway, so we'd go home and crawl into bed with a book or our girl- or boyfriends.

Besides sex and gossip, the main form of entertainment on the Ranch was reading. It was not Osho who was the most widely read author, but a guy named Louis L'Amour, who'd written eighty-some Western novels. Everybody was reading them, not only us wanna- be cowboys, but also those tender mas. The novels provided the perfect dreams for the physical environment we were living in.

It was always really the same story. The dudes would ride around on the range, prospect for gold, rustle some cattle and sit around campfires, drinking coffee that was "black as sin and strong enough to float a horseshoe". The bad guys were pursued through deserts and canyons, and finally would meet their fate in page-long fist- and gun-fights. The good guys would always triumph in the end and ride off into the sunset, a beautiful woman by their side. Well-told, simple stories that would go in and out without leaving any damage, and we loved them.

The paperbacks were passed around from hand to hand and there seemed to be an endless supply. During my first two years on the Ranch I must have made it through more than 150

Western novels. Then came a point where that genre seemed to have exhausted itself. I went through a brief identity crisis, and then graduated to thrillers and adventure novels (which is still my preferred reading material today).

***

-28-

We would soon enough find out what it meant to be in a "crunch", when due to certain deadlines the workload was increased significantly. The working hours were extended, sometimes to 14 or more hours a day, the whole commune shifted into a different gear and individually as well as communally we were pushed to the limit.

In the spring of 1982 the announcement was made that in July, for "Master's Day" (also known as "Guru Poornima", a traditional Indian festival held on the full moon of that month), we were going to host the "First Annual World Celebration", and that we were expecting between ten and fifteen thousand visitors. Wow. All those people had to stay somewhere and had to be taken care of, food, transportation, entertainment, the works. And they were not just any people, they were our friends from around the world, and they'd come for the same reason that we were here for, to be with Osho. No, this wasn't going to be just a humpty-dumpty job, we were going to do it like we were doing everything else – in a totally professional manner, and with a lot of love.

During the spring, when the weather had gotten warmer, scores of "summer workers" had joined us at the Ranch. They were sannyasins mainly from the States, but also from European centers, that were staying in tents for the summer to help with the work. Without them, we couldn't have done it. The preparations for the festival were started on many different fronts at the same time. Since I was working in construction, that is the angle from which I saw what was going on.

We purchased what must have been four or five thousand tents, each large enough for three persons, plus foam mattresses and sleeping bags. In a huge, backbreaking operation we built a corresponding amount of sturdy, wooden tent platforms, which were then trucked to the tent sites that in the meantime had been carefully surveyed. Dozens of people worked for weeks to carry them to their place and, with the help of wooden legs, raise them off the ground and level them. That was no small feat since some of the tent sites were way up in picturesque side valleys that were not accessible to motor vehicles. And the platforms were all meticulously squared up against each other, each in a certain distance from the next ones, row after perfectly straight row.

Meanwhile, I was working with a crew (the "Pipelina Pipe Crew", named after a joke that Osho had once told - there was this guy Luigi, an Italian immigrant, who was telling his friends about his work, and they were starting to wonder who this "Pipelina" was that was getting laid by so many guys ... until they found out that it was not a woman, but a pipeline) that was laying mile after mile of eight- and twelve-inch pipes for a water and sewer system. First we'd have a backhoe dig a four to five foot trench, then we'd spread a layer of gravel at the bottom, join the sections of pipe together, and finally the trench was backfilled by a front-end loader.

After a few weeks of that I joined the "blocking crew". Several dozen shower- and toilet trailers had been rolled in next to the tent sites. They needed to be set on cinderblock piers so that their wheels were off the ground. For weeks we'd crawl around underneath those trailers, schlepp heavy cinderblocks and stack them into piers.

"Niggering", we'd call that kind of work with our typical mischievous sannyasin humor that wouldn't stop at anything. With the help of pneumatic jacks we'd lift a corner of the trailer a bit higher than it needed to be, built the pier there up to the necessary height, then lower the trailer down onto it. That procedure was repeated for each of the dozen or so piers a trailer needed to safely sit on. And of course, the sucker had to be dead level. Then it could be hooked up to the pipes that we had laid earlier.

It felt like coming to a holiday camp when we eventually moved on to build a number of burlap-covered shade areas, complete with tables and benches made of cinderblocks and planks, that were going to be next to snack bars.

More often than not during that time I walked home after dinner, on wobbly knees and with aching shoulders, totally tuckered out. And sometimes I was wondering what the festival was going to be like, and whether anybody was going to come in the first place.

In late June, I was doing one of my weekly night shifts at Mahakashyap Reception. That was before we had any kind of security on the Ranch. I was the only person there awake throughout the night, to take any phone calls that might be coming in, and to be generally available for anything that might happen (and nothing ever did). Except during that night, right in front of my eyes, bus after bus after bus came rolling in, all of them full of travel-weary festival participants from all over the world. Boy, they were really coming! With tears in my eyes I waved at them (and some who did see me even waved back) and I realized that finally the party could begin.

The festival turned out to be a huge success. All in all, about thirteen thousand guests came, and of all the festivals that we were ever going to have on the Ranch that was probably the most magical one. Osho sat with us in silence for six morning satsangs and an evening darshan on Guru Poornima Day. For many of us this was the first time in over a year to see him, and for many more it was the first time ever to be in his presence.

The end of the festival meant good-bye to all our friends that had come, heartbreak city. The commune shifted down a gear, and we started to take everything down that we'd put up for the celebration. We were also confronted with the fact that summer was going to be over before we'd know it, and that we still needed much more permanent housing. The "summer workers" couldn't possibly stay on in their tents once the weather got really cold and wet. We'd need to come up with a way where we could construct our own housing on a large scale. And it had to be relatively economical. To just continue to bring in prefabricated homes was simply too expensive in the long run.

Then somebody had a glorious idea. We still had all those tent platforms that by now were stored in a side valley, pile upon pile upon pile. So we took three platforms and nailed them together to form a triangle, with one platform as the floor and the other two as the roof. A front wall was put in with a door, and a rear wall with a window. Then we added roofing shingles, insulation, electrical wiring and fixtures, interior paneling and wall-to-wall carpeting on the floor and, bingo, an "A-frame" cabin was born.

In an assembly-line type operation we cranked out what must have amounted to two or three hundred A-frames and set them up in a beautiful valley called Walt Whitman Grove, along with toilet and shower trailers that we still had from the festival. And the first ones of them were ready to be inhabited some time in the fall, just in time. Another site, Alan Watts Grove, was graced with a later, more advanced creation, "Quadruplexes", that combined four A-frames with a set of bathrooms between them.

***

-29-

By then, our situation in Oregon had become increasingly difficult. A lot of people really liked us, and a lot of them didn't and were more and more active about it. Government officials became uncooperative or outright hostile. A land-use watchdog group, the "1,000 Friends of Oregon" challenged the incorporation of our city in court. Neighbors, churches and others started to raise a lot of stink. And some of us in a position to do so certainly did their share to provoke more of all that.

One of our neighbors across Radha River was a guy named Bill Bowerman who owned a ranch there (and his son owned another one right next to it). He was a famous track coach and in some function associated with the athletic shoe- and apparel- maker Nike (who have their international headquarters in Oregon). For whatever reason, Bowerman hated our guts, and he exerted enough influence on Nike so that over the years they donated thousands and thousands of dollars against our cause. (Keep that in mind when you go out to buy your next pair of sneakers, whether MJ's your hero or not.)

During that time, I left the Ranch only on rare occasions. I continued to bang nails in construction, and that whole aspect of our life appeared to be rather remote. At the most, it was a subject for gossip at tea time, or a form of entertainment, when I'd read the press clippings about us that were pinned by the dozens on our communal bulletin board.

Yes, the press loved us. In fact, for the *Oregonian* in Portland, the largest daily paper in the state, we were the "number one newsmaker", and that for three consecutive years, 1983 to 1985. There was seldom an issue without a story on "the Bhagwan" and his "red-clad followers", often on the front page. Facts, rumors, fiction or any combination thereof, it was printed and gobbled up by the readers.

I dare say that nobody, journalists, readers or even the residents at the Ranch, knew or understood what was *really* going on there. Only Osho might have been able to provide that answer, and he was in silence. And at least as far as he was concerned, he never cared about whether he was getting "good press" or not - as long as they were writing. (What does the moon care if a dog barks at it?)

What I did notice though, on occasion, was what kind of people would come down to visit. "Martians", we called them, because they certainly stuck out in their clothes that were predominantly colored in shades of blue or grey. The road that led down to the Ranch and continued onwards to eventually leave our property again was a county road and therefore public. Anybody could use it, but only the road itself. It was up to us, the owners, to allow someone to go off the side of the road onto our property.

And enough Oregonians apparently showed enough interest or curiosity in us to drive down for a look-see. There were battered pick-up trucks driven by angry-looking rednecks, shotguns clearly visible in their racks, and with bumper stickers reading, "Better dead than red". There was a panel truck that showed up quite frequently, with large signs attached to the sides with bible quotes warning us of what would await us on judgment day ("The wages of sin are death!"). I met nice, open people that were genuinely interested in what we were doing. I saw folks that seemed rather timid, looked around suspiciously and avoided contact. And as best as I could I tried to steer clear of those Christian fundamentalists that stood there with bibles under their arms, trying to engage anybody they could get a hold of into a conversation to save their souls. Yeah, praise the Lord, that certainly increased the entertainment value of downtown Rajneeshpuram.

It was also during that time that we were starting to get buzzed by overflying fighter jets. At first they came only occasionally, eventually as often as a few times a week. One of their favorite visiting times would be right around drive-by. They were flying so low that we could clearly see the pilots in their cockpits.

We checked out where their designated flight corridors were, and, indeed, those pilots had strayed way off course. Our complaints to the authorities were of no avail. It very much looked like somebody was pulling some strings with the US Air Force.

***

-30-

Back in Poona, the commune had been basically run by women; that was the way Osho wanted it. And this was even more so the case on the Ranch. Even in fields that by their very nature were rather male-dominated, like construction or heavy machinery, women were put in charge, and soon there was going to be no place where you could be safe from them. Chuang Tzu was even run jointly by two mas, who were quite busy pushing each other's buttons, on top of everybody else's.

The construction crews had initially been all male. At some point, one token ma was assigned to each crew, and the swamis, many of whom were quite happy living out any macho-trips they might have left, didn't quite know what to do with them (except for maybe the occasional nooner in the bushes). So the mas were sent up to Maggie's to rustle up supplies for the tea breaks, to run errands or maybe to clean some tools. Once we'd gotten used to our "tea moms", more and more mas were sent to join the crews, and we could not help but to actually give them tools and teach them some of the tricks of the trade. That did not happen without creating a lot of confusion and challenging the self-esteem of us tough construction guys. Still, it proved to be a splendid device to mellow us out some and to increase our awareness of how we were dealing with one another.

And then, there was Ma Anand Sheela. In Poona, she had been Laxmi's assistant, who then had been Osho's secretary. On the Ranch, Sheela was The Queen. She was running the show, if necessary, with an iron fist, and she'd go and see Osho every evening for whatever guidance was needed. I have met Sheela on some occasions, and she came across as a very beautiful and gentle woman. But she also had another side to her, that of a prize bitch, tough as nails, totally outrageous and off the wall. It was her practical, hands-on approach to things that was one of the key ingredients for the amazingly smooth functioning of the commune.

She was surrounded by an entourage of women that had more or less the same qualities. All of them were obviously people you did not want to cross. That applied to commune members as well as to outside people. There was a government official who'd had dealings with some of them and who reportedly said that he'd never in his life come across a meaner and nastier bunch of bitches. Some compliment! But they sure as hell got the job done, for better or worse. In the "us-against-them" world that was developing it was certainly an asset to have them on our side, however much they'd been instrumental to create that situation in the first place.

Every couple of weeks, there was a commune meeting with Sheela, typically at Maggie's after dinner. In grand style, she'd come sweeping in with a few of her cronies in tow and take over the show. As an appetizer, she told some Osho stories that we all loved and that got everybody's attention, and went on to news and gossip from our commune and the sannyas world at large. She also could get quite personal with people she obviously had an ax to grind with. Jayananda, her husband, was ridiculed and ripped apart. Then there was this person who was a total blockhead, and that person had fucked up royally. For over an hour she'd go on, ranting and raving, administering verbal spankings left, right and center, dishing out piles of wit and shit.

Normally, I enjoyed the first 15 or 20 minutes of it, then became more and more bored, upset that I had to sit there and suffer through the whole thing. But I could not just get up and leave. No way.

So I decided to quit going. When a meeting was to be held, I'd sneak out after dinner, go home and have a quiet evening with myself. That strategy worked for quite a while. At some point they started to have everybody sign their name on a list before the beginning of the meeting. Still, I was able to fake that one. I'd put down my name as early as it was possible, and then slip out quietly and head for home.

Then one fateful day the meeting was not held at Maggie's, but at the airport hangar, after dinner. Fuck that, I said to myself. Except a couple of days later I got a note to come down to Sheela's trailer the next day, 10 am sharp. I went and was ushered into a room where there were about 20 other people waiting, and we all had one thing in common. Guess what. Somebody at some office must have taken the attendance list of the meeting and run it against a master list of the commune residents, quite a job, and with obvious results. The mood in the room was rather subdued, and that increased significantly when Vidya, one of Sheela's heavyweights, entered, and the massacre began. She knew every one of us, under which circumstances we had come, even some details of our history as a sannyasin that we thought was long forgotten. She had an uncanny ability to read our defenses and slash through them and she proceeded in whichever way she could get through to us. Some of us with apparently thick skins got a bit more of a rap, others less. What all of us wanted the least was to get kicked out of the commune, and that threat was used in some cases rather openly, in others more veiled.

By the time she came to me, I was sitting there crouched in my corner, more in the wall itself than leaning against it, scared shitless. My excuse why I had not come to the meeting was that I had not heard the announcement - there had been so much noise at my construction site that I had been wearing protective earmuffs. Whether she believed that or not, she probably saw by the state I was in that she'd already succeeded in driving her point home, and I got away with a warning. None of us actually got kicked out, but we were all pretty much demolished. Was this shock therapy, or what? Sweet Lord, I got out of there, shaking in my boots, and I humbly went back to work.

I did learn one very important lesson that day: don't fuck with the authorities. Or rather, when you do, proceed with a lot of caution. They have a lot of power that they can use against you, and, as far as I'm concerned, I don't necessarily feel like becoming a martyr. I'm not advertising here that anybody should become a spineless aye-sayer. This doesn't necessarily have anything to do with how much integrity I've got. My first responsibility is towards myself, and there is a fine, but distinct line between telling someone who is standing on my foot to get off and putting something at risk that is of much greater importance to me than testing my "power" against somebody else's.

Moreover, for my further life on the Ranch (and after) I learned that when I was confronted with something that I, for whatever reason, did not like or agree with, then I should not avoid it, but face it, while keeping an inner distance to it. I can practise that on anything that I'd encounter in life, and the result is a more peaceful inner being. (Still practising, by the way!)

When I look back now at some of the "devices" that were used at the Ranch, I cannot say that it is up to me to judge something as right or wrong. Whatever happens, happens for a reason, and nothing happens to me unless I've had it coming. Life is incredibly fair that way. There are no accidents, ever. I may not know the whole story, that's another thing. And after all, "truth is what works". The name of the game is to wake up, and not to get onto any morality trip. I've come across a lot of people that are incredibly hung up about what a spiritual seeker (or master, for that matter) should be like, and that image is more oriented on those so-called Christian saints or fakes like Mother Theresa than on how reality really works. To me, it is more important to be true to myself, and to whatever any given moment might demand, whether that is "good" or "bad". I'd rather be authentic than a phony, and let the chips fall where they may. Sure, it sounds nice to create "good" karma with "good" deeds, but karma is karma, and what I really want to do is to get out of the whole wheel and wake up.

***

-31-

One of the most memorable jobs that I ever had on the Ranch was that as a mouse catcher at B-Site. It was always a treat to be near Osho's trailer. The energy was noticeably thicker there, and just by spending a bit of time there you'd get a good shot of vitamin B. In the early days, we could go up and sit on the lawn in front of his house and greet him there when he'd come out for his drive. Later, there were more and more of us and the area was generally off-limits, unless, in rare cases, you had some work to do there.

However, it was not only us that found that energy field extremely attractive. Hordes of field mice from the surrounding hills were invading the site, and they were causing a lot of damage to the buildings there. So, practical as we were, we set up a line of traps underneath Osho's trailer, and those needed to be serviced.

For about half a year, twice a week, I'd go up to B-Site with another swami while Osho was out for his daily spin. Equipped with knee-pads and flashlights, we'd get into the crawl space underneath the trailer to collect the traps. We crawled out again, disposed of the dead mice (they very unceremoniously went into a garbage bin for compost), cleaned the traps, baited them with peanut butter (yummy!) and went back underneath to set them up again. And, high as a kite, we went back to our regular jobs.

While we were at B-Site to take care of the mice we also had an opportunity to catch a glimpse of the Rolls-Royces that were sitting there, dozens of them, so many we didn't even have enough garage space for them. They were owned by the "Rajneesh Modern Car Collection Trust", all of them the same basic model, a Silver Spur. We had somebody there who would do a very professional paint job on them, and the sky was the limit. Not two of them were of the same color. Some were more plain and stately looking, others were glittering in gold and silver. A few came psychedelically multi-colored, a number of them had beautiful pictures painted on them, with landscapes, animals, sunsets or rainbows. My favorite was one that seemed to be engulfed in flames. And every day Osho would come out for his ride in a different one. At times we'd wage bets while we were waiting for him by the side of the road, and sometimes there were cheers and applause from us when he'd show up in a particularly outrageous looking one. We all loved it, and so did he.

There was also still the "original" Rolls that had been shipped over from India, somewhat larger in size, in plain white and bullet-proof. That model was used when Osho came to sit with us during the celebrations, and on those occasions he was chauffeured.

In the end, we had ninety-three Rolls-Royces there, and the way I see it, it was all a big, practical, in-your-face joke. If you consider how car-crazy particularly America is, Osho took that obsession *ad absurdum*. It was one of his ways where he'd blow some people's minds on how a spiritual master should behave. (He also used devices like that to weed out people that were with him for the wrong reasons.) What he really did, like in so many other ways, was to hold a mirror in front of our face. And not all of us liked the reflection that we saw and, instead of looking at the source of the reflection, started to blame the mirror. He was amazingly creative when it came to utilizing just about anything for this game. Not everybody was able to take that, and it caused a lot of trouble for him and his commune.

***

"Top of the Ranch", ca. 1984

Osho at Lao Tzu Grove

Drive-by, festival-time

Building pathways in Walt Whitman Grove, late 1982

A-frame factory, late 1982

Devateerth Mall under construction, ca. 1984

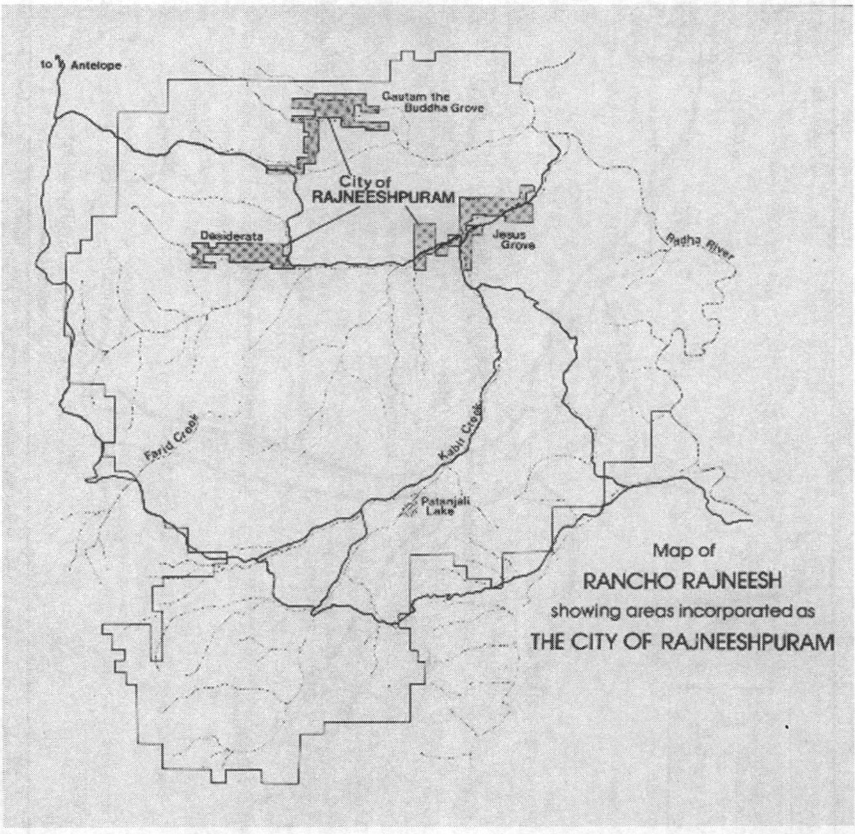

Map of
RANCHO RAJNEESH
showing areas incorporated as
THE CITY OF RAJNEESHPURAM

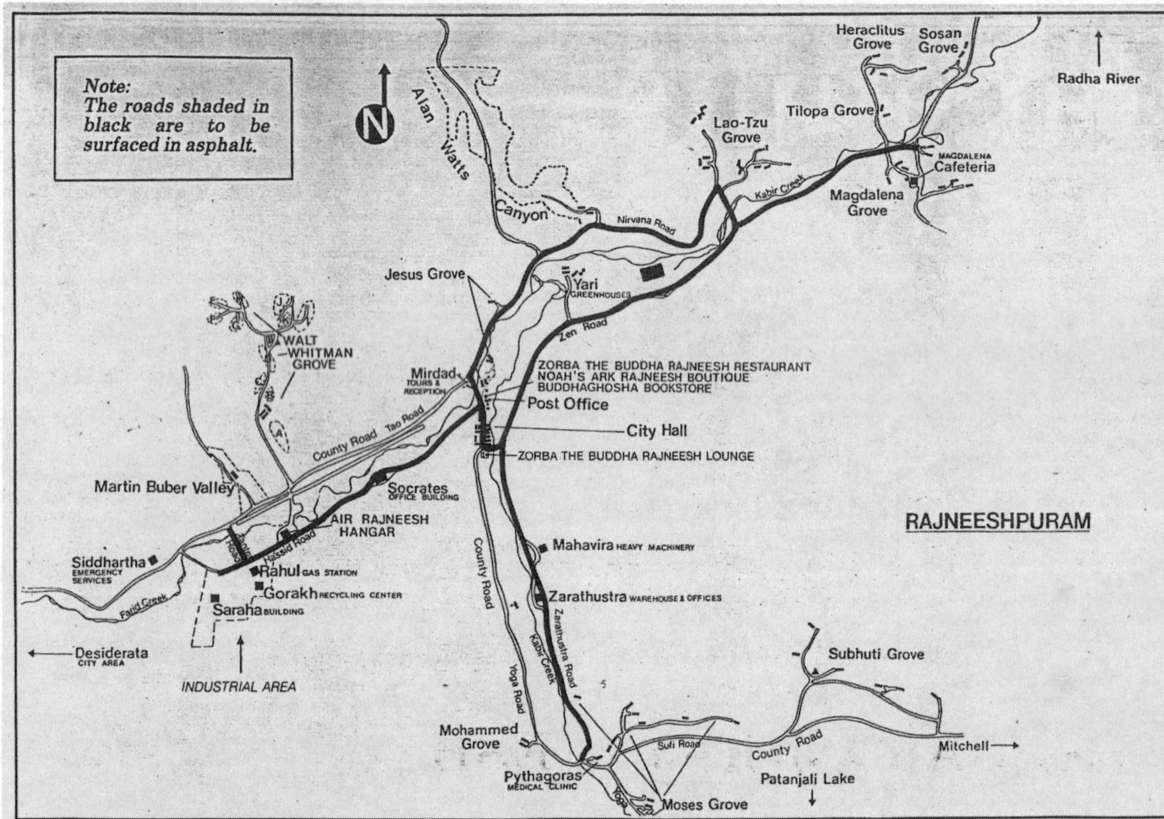
Note:
The roads shaded in black are to be surfaced in asphalt.
N
Alan Watts Canyon
Heraclitus Grove
Sosan Grove
Radha River
Tilopa Grove
Lao-Tzu Grove
MAGDALENA Cafeteria
Magdalena Grove
Kabir Creek
Nirvana Road
Jesus Grove
Yari GREENHOUSES
Zen Road
WALT WHITMAN GROVE
Mirdad TOURS & RECEPTION
ZORBA THE BUDDHA RAJNEESH RESTAURANT
NOAH'S ARK RAJNEESH BOUTIQUE
BUDDHAGHOSHA BOOKSTORE
Post Office
City Hall
ZORBA THE BUDDHA RAJNEESH LOUNGE
County Road
Tao Road
Martin Buber Valley
Socrates OFFICE BUILDING
AIR RAJNEESH HANGAR
RAJNEESHPURAM
Hassid Road
Siddhartha EMERGENCY SERVICES
Rahul GAS STATION
Gorakh RECYCLING CENTER
Saraha BUILDING
Farid Creek
Mahavira HEAVY MACHINERY
Zarathustra WAREHOUSE & OFFICES
Zarathustra Road
Desiderata CITY AREA
INDUSTRIAL AREA
Yoga Road
Subhuti Grove
Mohammed Grove
Sufi Road
County Road
Mitchell
Pythagoras MEDICAL CLINIC
Patanjali Lake
Moses Grove

Downtown Rajneeshpuram with festival tents

Magdalena Cafeteria, aka Maggie's Cafe

The Lao Tzu townhouses, ca. 1984

-32-

Although we were receiving an increasing amount of hate- mail and threats, it had not come to outright violence, except that commune members going off the Ranch were often met with jeers or hostile vibes, and that road signs leading to our property were used for target practice.

Then, in August 1983, an actual bomb exploded. In Portland we were operating a hotel that was mainly used as a stop-over by visitors going to or coming from the Ranch, or by commune members who were in town on some business. Some guy had checked into the hotel, supposedly on his way to the Ranch. He had a self-fabricated explosive device with him that went off in his room, mutilating both of his hands. "Stubby", as we'd call him, was arrested and eventually went to court, but never to jail. However, the incident sent shockwaves through the commune. Something had to be done to forestall further activities like that.

Up to that point, security on the Ranch had been minimal. We had sent a couple of people to a police academy that were forming the nucleus of a small municipal "Peace Force" for the City of Rajneeshpuram. But they never knew who might be out there when they'd go on a patrol late at night. It went far beyond the scope of their work to sufficiently monitor who'd be coming down the county road and who might be trespassing onto our property.

Hence, "Rajneesh Security" was formed, a private security service run by "Rajneesh Neo-Sannyas International Commune" ("RNSIC" - which was legally a different entity than the City). I was among the first wave of commune members that were "drafted". At first we were more or less sitting out in the wind and the rain, but soon small guard huts were built for us, equipped with two-way radios, telephones and, of course, coffee percolators.

On the "Hill" leading down to the Ranch we had four posts: the "Top of the Ranch" at the entrance of the property, then Buddha Grove, Desiderata Canyon and Gurdjieff Dam. There were five more posts at the actual Ranch, wherever a private road would lead off the county road. Lastly, there was a post way out at the truck farm, overlooking Radha River (that post was always a great place to catch up on your reading). All the posts had code names, and those were changed from time to time. At times it was Western heroes we were using, at times planets and stars, or cartoon characters ("Snoopy to Batman, come in please!").

What we were doing was to monitor the coming and going of non-Ranch vehicles and to be on the alert for anything odd or potentially dangerous. And we were doing that with as much professionalism as possible.

I wonder how it must have sounded to an outsider when we were communicating with each other on the air, passing on the license plates of cars and their encoded descriptions and other information. Actually, in a small town many miles away there was a bar where they were receiving our transmissions (we did have a quite powerful relay station), and the clientele there would sip their Budweisers while listening to the Rajneeshies doing their crazy number. I mean, it was pretty obvious what it was all about, and it probably did anything but increase our good standing with the local yokels.

We were operating the posts 24 hours a day, seven days a week, in rotating shifts. After a week, we'd change shifts and move on to another post. Each post was a different story, depending on its location and on the particular duties assigned to it within the whole game. There was only one guard at most of the Ranch posts, while on the Hill it was always a swami and a ma. Once during each shift, a car would come around to all the posts to bring food and snacks. No, we certainly were not starving, on the contrary.

A lot of the time it was pretty much relaxed, at other times incredibly intense, for instance when there was a lot of traffic. On the Hill posts it was always very crucial who your partner was. With some, I just had a wonderful time and we both were sad to move on after our week was over, with others I went through a week of hell.

And we had all kinds of little games going to make our life more fun, particularly on the Hill. We told our lifetime stories countless times, played battleships and gave Tarot readings to each other. One of us was a mathematician, and he spent the night shifts working on complex algebraic equations. In early summer, we soon found out that the sunflower seeds in our trail mix were still live, so all the Hill posts started elaborate gardens, and by late summer the guard huts were dwarfed by gigantic sunflowers. Squirrels, chipmunks, mice and other small critters living in the vicinity of the huts were growing quite fat. Our mascot was Fred, a lone coyote who had the habit of wandering along the county road and would sometimes make it all the way down to the Ranch. He'd pass the Top, the guys there would get on the radio, and, sure enough, guess who'd show up at Buddha Grove half an hour later.

On occasion, we'd add a good dose of humor to our radio transmissions. One of us pulled off whole talk shows on the radio during night shifts that were so incredibly funny that we were almost rolling on the floor with laughter … and all that while staying totally alert, of course. (Before long, the "office" got wind of that, and word came down that any communication on the radio was to be limited to crisp professional talk.) And one of the great pleasures during the summer was to stop at Krishnamurti Lake for a swim in the early morning after a night shift on the Hill, before going home to sleep.

There were quite a few of us that just hated to be in security. I didn't mind, really, and for the most part made the best of it and quite enjoyed myself hanging out in those little huts. Still, after almost a year and a half there, it started to wear me down a bit, particularly the week of night shifts that would come along once a month. However, to go and ask for a job change might have disastrous consequences, so I stayed put.

Then, one evening in January 1985, myself and the other people on my shift were riding up to the security office in our old, beat-up station wagon (it was nicknamed "Heavy Metal" and was badly smelling of fish). This was going to be our seventh and last graveyard shift of a cycle. To some extent, we were all tired of it and were indulging in a little bitching and complaining, and in that mood came up with the idea to entertain everybody with a little prank during our shift. It were the "radio checks" that were to be the object of our frustration. During times when there was not a lot of radio traffic, every hour the security office ("Hollywood") would do a radio check with the posts, and with all of them, one after the other.

"Hollywood to Jupiter, come in please."

"Jupiter here, go ahead."

"This is a radio check. How do you read me?"

"You're coming in loud and clear."

"10-4. Over and out."

And on to the next one. Since all of the Ranch posts were using the same channel (and the Hill posts a different one), that meant that you had to listen to a lot of talking that wasn't necessarily very interesting, mildly put. Especially during the night, when nothing was going on, these radio checks became a constant source of irritation. You might not want to listen to the crap, but you had no other choice.

So we said, OK, let's just ignore the radio check after 2 am and remain silent, and with that went off to start our shift.

Soon it was 2 am, Hollywood came on the air, and nobody answered. We were all sitting in our huts, giggling away, and were admittedly feeling a little sorry for that poor ma at the office who was starting to show a bit of concern in her vain attempts to raise us. She soon enough changed her strategy though and got on the phone to make sure we were all alive and well, and made it clear that she had not enjoyed her part in our little game one single bit.

The next morning we had our weekly security meeting. Naturally, one of the main topics was a certain incident that had happened during the previous night. We were sternly reminded that something like that was an absolute no-no and to better behave ourselves in the future, or else. Us sinners ruefully agreed, and then went home to sleep.

Early in the afternoon, I was awoken by a swami who came into my room to give me an urgent message to come to an important meeting at some office at the Ranch. Well, what could that be? I didn't make the connection until I showed up there and found myself in the company of my co-conspirators of the night before. It started to look very much as if the lesson Vidya had given me about two years before was getting a refresher. This time it was Nirmal who read to us from The Book, and she did a pro job. She skillfully took every one of us completely apart and then left us there to dry. We were summarily expelled from security and were sent to work at Magdalena Cafeteria. This was meant as a punishment - off to "Maggie's Farm" (remember that old Dylan-song?), and, by all means, it was anything but an "honorable discharge".

For a day or two, I was walking around like in a haze, in total shock. And we were the talk of the commune. Friends came up to me and said, "Bo, I never thought you'd pull off a number like that!" The feedback I got was overwhelmingly sympathetic, almost with a touch of admiration, and one swami even remarked, "God, if I'd only known that something like that would get me out of security!"

At Maggie's, I wasn't sent to chop veggies or to scrub pots and pans, as I had feared. Since I was able-bodied and still had a good back I joined an old buddy of mine on the loading dock and had a marvelous time. After all those months of inertia, my body was just dying to move. Moreover, in the storage trailers there were all kinds of goodies like boxes of chocolate and raisins. We were munching so much stuff that we had hardly any appetite left for the regular meals. Unfortunately, this lasted only about three weeks, when I got another job change, this time to Chaitanya, the accounts department.

***

-33-

The commune around Osho has always been an extremely dynamic place. Changes were implemented all the time, you can almost say religiously, or seemed to happen on their own accord in that high-energy environment. They were seen as the perfect antidote to get us out of any habit, old or new, and to help focus us on the present moment. Despite of all the chaos and confusion that came along with that, the commune was always functioning like a well-oiled, efficient and smoothly running machine.

There was a considerable amount of discipline, where it was needed, but we were also given much more freedom to be ourselves and to follow our heart than I have experienced anywhere out in the "world". The system was always so flexible that ultimately you ended up where you needed to be, and everything that needed to get done did get done, and done well.

By and large, I had always felt that the way things were being done was the same way I would have done myself, if it had been up to me to decide. In the last year or so, however, a number of changes had happened where I was starting to wonder a bit about where we were heading. It was not that it created a problem for me. Osho was here, and so was I, and I knew how I felt about him.

That was what counted. Everything else was of secondary importance, more on the periphery of things. And I had learned to be a lot more accepting of matters that were beyond my scope of understanding or influence. Still, there were certain instances where, somewhere inside, I was raising an eyebrow, so to speak. I might not say anything, but notice I did.

A political, or rather, spiritual correctness was creeping up, where it was "on" to use certain expressions and absolutely "off" to utter others. The "moms", as our coordinators were now called, were closely watching that everybody complied. It went as far as that it was "off" to refer to our grub place as "Maggie's". No, the name was "Magdalena Cafeteria". Still, if you were wise enough, you could use all that as a vehicle for your personal growth, like just about anything else, however much "off" it appeared.

In many ways, we started to behave more like an organized, established religion, very much in contrast to the spontaneous and earthy spirituality that had become something like a trademark for being a sannyasin. We were now officially registered as a church, and thousands of copies of a small booklet were printed, an introduction to the "religion" of "Rajneeshism", edited by the "Academy of Rajneeshism". New publications of Osho's discourses were published by "Bodhisattvaa Ma Anand Sheela, M.M., D.Phil.M., D.Litt.M.(RIMU), Acharya". Other sannyasins, like the editors, were sporting similar titles. Sheela herself was running around in a costume looking like the pope, and that guy certainly had never been a role model for us. Everywhere on the Ranch, before and after work, we were kneeling down and doing the "Gachchamis" (originally a very beautiful Buddhist chant we first started using in 1981 when Osho had given his May satsangs), after someone had given the "reminders". Work departments became "temples", the work itself became "worship".

Sure, on some level we were trying to make it harder for certain elements in the outside world to get to us, and that was by declaring everything that we were doing as being part of our religion. Hey, that was the case, anyway, but the outer form it took did feel a bit off.

And then, there were the guns, handguns as well as Uzis, and quite a few of them. Our "Peace Force" had always been equipped with revolvers, as it is customary in America, and nobody ever saw anything wrong in that. In security, we were not armed. But at some point another outfit came into being, consisting mainly of guys (and even some ladies) that appeared to be somewhat closely connected to Sheela. When I was on security duty at Buddha Grove, they would regularly drive past on their way to some remote spot to do target practice. They were the same people that were in the lead vehicle during drive-by, as well as in the follow-up vehicle, with Uzis in plain sight.

At the drive-bys during the festivals, when there were big crowds lining up to greet Osho, Sheela was around helping with the organizing, with a gun on her hip. Around B-Site there was now a high chain-link fence and an armed guard at the entrance. And what broke many people's hearts was that during satsangs there would be a heavily armed guard positioned on each side of Osho's podium. Was all that really needed as a deterrent, or was someone becoming a bit paranoid?

***

-34-

On October 30, 1984, Osho started speaking again. On a daily basis, he'd give discourses to a small group of disciples called "The Chosen Few", who were "going to be the messengers of Rajneeshism for the world at large". Never mind that line, this was really exciting. Each discourse was videotaped and then shown the next evening on a giant screen to all of us at Rajneesh Mandir, our huge gathering place for satsangs and meditations.

Once, a discourse was not shown. The official word was that the video camera had screwed up, but as later leaked out, Osho had made some very strong and disapproving remarks concerning the management of the commune.

As a resident, I was invited to attend a live discourse every few weeks. They were held in a relatively small room up at B-Site, and it was very important to come dressed warmly, since it was freezing cold in there. Osho may have been a hot master, but he certainly enjoyed quite low temperatures in the locations he was living in.

About the same time, another nice gig started to happen. During his drives up the county road and onwards to the small town of

Madras, Osho had been hassled several times by locals that were taking the opportunity to show their dislike with what was happening at the Ranch.

He had also gotten a couple of speeding tickets, and once he was involved in an accident with a cement truck – not through his fault, and he was not harmed – and had to be taken back in the lead vehicle.

In months of hard work, we built our own road for him, on our own property. "Mevlana Bhagwan Road" was going up many miles past Patanjali Lake into a remote corner of our land, and he had it all to himself. Residents and long-term commune workers - oops! I mean "worshippers" – were invited periodically to go out and greet him where he would turn around at the end of the road before driving back.

So, two or three times a month I'd pile into a van with another half-dozen people some time before drive-by. A short distance before our destination, we'd leave the road, continue a ways up a dirt track, leave our car, and hike up a slope for about half a mile before we'd get to the turnaround to line up and wait. Soon enough, he came cruising up the road. Yes, obviously he loved to drive. He handled the car with his usual grace, and looked pretty cool wearing his designer sunglasses. We got our namaste, and then he was gone again, and the hills around us were as silent as ever.

It wasn't that the new commune was everybody's cup of tea. The way I see it is that when it is right for you to be with the master, then it happens. Then existence is totally supportive, in many mysterious ways, against all odds. When it is not your time, then any small incident can become the excuse to leave. It was never easy to be around Osho. We all had our own reasons to be there, or to go, and the door was always open. I hope that doesn't come across as too self-righteous. I can really only speak for myself, and not for others, whose whole story I don't know. Over the years, I've seen many people come and go, including myself, and each story is different.

Many of my old friends from Poona joined the communes in Europe, coming to the Ranch for the festivals or for longer, but limited stays. Many others never made it, for whatever reason, and I'd never see them again.There were people that were residents at the Ranch that at some point decided to go.

I remember a swami, an ashramite for many years, who came to the Ranch and was put to work on a front-end loader. After a week, he called it quits and left for Goa (of all places!). Another old- timer, a very soft guy who still wore his hair long and was walking around in Tai-Chi shoes was sent to clean trailers and disappeared after a few days. A good friend of mine, who I'd done a wonderful week with in security, decided that it was time for her to "go and play out in the world". One of the writers for the Rajneesh Times didn't want to put up any more with what he was told to write and left, shaken up and in tears.

A few people were spooked by what was happening around Sheela and drove out in the middle of the night. And then there was the swami whose job it was to be the Fire Chief. Driving around in that flashy fire engine of ours was a very high profile job with many privileges, and the mas were flocking to his feet. One day he went to Jesus Grove and asked for a job change, and promptly was sent to join the cement crew. He lasted less than two weeks before tossing the towel.

Some people were very clear about where they needed to be and left in good standing, others turned weird or negative. A deciding factor for who was at the Ranch and who not was certainly also the way an individual was viewed by the management, whether they liked him or her or not. Quite a few members of the old Ashram establishment were obviously seen as a threat by Sheela and her crew and treated very rudely, and some of them were never allowed to come. A friend of mine, a sweet and gentle ma who had been living in Lao Tzu House back in Poona, was bullied around for some time ("gang-banged", as she called it) until she gave up and left.

People that had "dropped" sannyas or had been excommunicated by the organization were now called "late sannyasins". Quite a few of those as well as others that had gotten disgruntled with the way things were going at the Ranch had settled in Santa Fe, New Mexico, and were jokingly referred to by us as "Camels", while some of them were calling themselves "The Wild Geese", who went as far as writing up some flyers directed against Sheela & Co. (Many years later, on a visit to Santa Fe, I found out that in fact there is a "Camel Rock" there, an imposing rock formation by the side of the road to Espanola.)

There were sannyasins, some of whom at one time had been very close to Osho, who did not shy away from turning against him publicly. One of them even wrote a rather dirty account about "the God that failed", which got published and was available at railroad station bookstalls all over India, and elsewhere. To me, that doesn't show an awful lot of spiritual integrity, to say the least. (In this case, it was the disciple that failed.)

As I said, I don't know the whole story of those people. But it made me sad to see them go. For me, they were part of that incredible thing that was happening around Osho, and for that I'd miss them ... and wish them well.

***

-35-

Meanwhile, life in the commune was continuing, business as usual, so to speak. While I was in security, I had largely missed the biggest crunch in the history of the Ranch, the town house crunch. In construction, we had gathered enough experience to tackle large-scale projects, and, starting in the fall of 1983 and continuing well into 1984, built the Lao Tzu town houses. They were located in a wide semi-circle, where B-Site opened up towards a relatively wide valley, in which Kabir Creek was running that came from the downtown area, past Rajneesh Mandir, to eventually pass Maggie's Cafe and then on to the truck farm and Radha River. We put up almost a hundred town houses, two-storey buildings, each with nine bedrooms, four bathrooms, four toilets and a living room with a small kitchen corner. It was a gigantic operation, and every hand that could be spared elsewhere was put to work.

Since security was considered a priority, I worked there only during relatively brief stints of "alternative worship", but still, I got a good taste. The site was bustling with activity, sometimes for periods of weeks with work days that went from 6 am to 10 pm.

During the same time, more or less, we built a hotel (with well over 100 rooms, all with attached bathrooms), a large two-storey mall building that stretched along the whole length of the downtown section of the county road ("Devateerth Mall"), with retail space downstairs and office space upstairs, and, for good measure, a number of smaller buildings, for storage and other purposes. And all that in addition to all the other buildings that had already been constructed. Our city was starting to take shape.

By the end of 1984, Rajneeshpuram had a downtown area that featured two restaurants, an ice cream parlor, Buddhagosha Bookstore for Osho's books, Omar Khayyam Bar, a post office, a bank, a travel bureau, a boutique, a gambling casino, and, last, but not least, a beauty parlor where residents could get free haircuts by top-notch hair stylists.

Of course, for a meal in a restaurant or a drink in the bar you needed money, and there were enough people here, residents or visitors, who apparently had enough of that. Like a lot of my friends there, I was more or less broke during my whole time on the Ranch, and money wasn't really needed, since for residents all the essentials were provided by the commune, for free. (That included even a pack of cigarettes a day.)

Elsewhere in the commune, the group department had turned into "Rajneesh International Meditation University" ("RIMU"), offering a wide array of groups, courses and sessions. After all, we had some of the top therapists and body workers in the world, and they were kept pretty busy. On a number of programs sponsored by the "Rajneesh Humanity Trust", sannyasins could come and participate in commune life for a few weeks or months.

All in all, in the summer of 1985, the number of residents and visitors had grown to between four and five thousand at any given time, about 2,000 of them "permanent" residents, and that was not counting the people who came by the thousands to our celebrations. What had once been a forlorn cattle ranch had turned into a flourishing small city.

We even had our own airport. Originally just a dirt strip where small craft could land, it was now a long tarmac runway, complete with landing lights, a hangar and an arrival and departure building. "Air Rajneesh" (Motto: "There is only one sky to fly in!") was flying to Portland on a regular schedule with its two seasoned convairs, and on the flights a couple of cute teenage mas were serving refreshments as stewardesses. A few times, I flew back to the Ranch from Portland after having done a week of security at the Hotel Rajneesh, and, looking down onto our city, was amazed how small it really was, compared to that big world outside.

***

-36-

On another front, though, trouble was brewing, and soon the shit was going to hit the fan, big time. The number of lawsuits we were engaged in had been growing steadily during the years. Government institutions, private persons and seemingly everybody else in Oregon were suing against us, for a multitude of reasons, and by mid-1985 we were involved in dozens of court cases. In May of that year I joined Rajneesh Legal Services ("RLS") as a paralegal, and there were more than 200 of us working there, taking care of the load.

A grand jury that had convened in Portland had been busy for a while, and by September it seemed imminent that they were coming down with some indictments. Obviously in anticipation of several arrests, Sheela and about 20 people of her "inner circle" packed their bags and left the Ranch for Germany on September 14. The commune was in shock. And the shocks continued as by and by a whole ton of stories came out about activities they had been engaged in behind our backs, activities not only directed against institutions and persons in the "outside world", but also against us. They clearly had misused the authority that had been entrusted to them. This definitely increased the energy level in the commune. We had called in the FBI and were investigating together with their agents (some of the alleged crimes were "federal" crimes, for instance wiretapping, besides arson and attempted murder and more), and on top of all that the Oregon National Guard had been mobilized, ready to invade should that be necessary. The pressure was becoming very intense.

Yet, we still had each other. I have to admit that at some point I started to wobble a bit, only to be told by a friend, "Hey, Bo, now's the time where you can show whether you're really a meditator or not!" Quite true. And above all, it was Osho, who stood up for his commune, whose tireless support prevented things from turning into chaos.

In the morning of October 28 I was just about to enter Maggie's for breakfast when I ran into my good buddy Satyena, who told me in as many words that Osho was in jail in Charlotte, North Carolina. I must have looked at him in total disbelief. "What the ... you've got to be kidding!" But he was not someone who would joke about such matters. It was the truth.

In the course of the next few hours more and more details emerged of what had happened. The day before, two rented Lear-jets had taken off from our airport with Osho and a few close disciples on board, and flown east across the continent. The "official" story was that he was going to take a vacation. Upon landing in Charlotte, Osho was arrested, at gunpoint and without a warrant, put in chains, and incarcerated in Mecklenburg County Jail.

What came down in the next twelve days is worth a book of its own, and is better to be told by someone with more of a legal and medical background than I have. We tried every legal strategy, every trick in the book to get him out of that jail, and to bring him back at least to Portland in such a way that his body would not be harmed. But the "authorities" kept on stonewalling. After all, they now held the trump card, him.

Eventually, on November 8, we managed to bring him home, and the drive-by upon his return was probably the most memorable in the history of the Ranch. The shock that we were still under was gradually replaced with a deep relief. At least for now, everything seemed to be all right again. We had him back.

It wasn't until much later that I began to understand the significance, the deeper meaning of what had happened. Osho was a master in playing the energy of the moment. With his move he had simply released pressure from a pot that was about to blow its lid off, he had defused a situation that had every potential to explode. We, his disciples, were clearly the beneficiaries. But he had paid a price that would have devastating effects on his health, and ultimately would prove to be fatal.

In the end, however, the City of Rajneeshpuram did not survive. The forces against us that wanted the commune destroyed were too formidable, and they included people in the highest levels of the Reagan administration (among them was the Attorney General at the time, Ed Meese). Their assessment that our weakest spot was Osho's immigration status proved to be correct, and eventually he had no choice but to leave the country. On November 14 we all saw him off at the Ranch airport. After a brief court hearing in Portland, he flew on to Delhi, India. It soon became clear to us that without him present we were not going to be able to continue and that we had to close down. And, considering what happened in Waco, Texas, a few years later, we had been relatively lucky that things turned out the way they did.

Some people left right away, others stayed on, some for months, to help with the chores that were still awaiting us to wind down our operation in an orderly way. So, where was I? With Osho gone, my main reason for being there had vanished. All my friends and everybody else were leaving by the busload, and it was only a matter of time before we'd all be gone. Where to go and what to do became the crucial question. No, I was not afraid or freaking out or thought that I had been dropped by existence that had been supporting me so beautifully. I did not feel betrayed by my master who, after all, had walked out on me for the second time. This was a beautiful opportunity to see where I was at with myself, a chance to apply what I had learned to "real" life, on my own. I had to be practical and focused on what needed to be done in the moment. Yes, I was pretty relaxed and in a good space, and I even started to look forward to what adventures might await me out there.

As could not be expected otherwise, Devika and I had been through some pretty heavy duty times with each other. We'd broken up, gotten together again, and finally broken up, seemingly for good. But towards the end of the Ranch we'd become good friends again and decided to make our start out in the world together. Her parents had moved to Santa Cruz, California, in the meantime and had offered that we could stay at their place until we found one of our own.

At the end of November, on Thanksgiving, I got on an outbound bus and saw the snow-covered hills of the Ranch for the last time. I did not cry, nor did I look back at that moment, but a big chunk of my heart will always be there.

***

-37-

Well, so what had it been all about, then? You can't say that we hadn't been warned. Way back in Poona, Osho had remarked at some point that the new commune was going to be "the biggest marketplace you've ever seen". Sure, we may have come with our own illusions. We were going to have a model commune, the envy of the New Age, where we'd all live blissfully until the end of our days, together with our master. And certainly we'd all get enlightened. What we got instead was a tough crash course in down-to-earth, basic spirituality, Osho-style. He had always had the knack to create situations in which we could learn, and this was one of them.

I can't remember any more what it all was that I went through. What remains today is more a certain taste. On the outside I might have looked radiant, but inside, most of the time, something or other was cooking. In a multitude of ways, I was thrown back upon myself, again and again and again, until I was reeling and hanging in the ropes, through devices that were anything but conventional. And so much more would have been possible had I been ready for it then. It was all given to me without me having to ask for it, a great gift, laid right into my lap.

Looking at it now from a certain distance makes the picture a bit clearer, but it still keeps evolving. Throughout the years, there have been things popping up that unquestioningly had received their share of work during the Ranch. Somewhere inside I am still digesting. Ultimately, Osho has given me my freedom, to the extent that I was able to receive it. Not a cheap, superficial freedom that gives me the license to do what I want to do out there, but a deeper, much more important freedom *from myself*, from having to do something in particular in the first place, that enables me more and more to just take what life decides to give to me and to let the river carry me to where it wants to.

I don't know how much Osho knew about what was going on in the commune, or why he didn't interfere. I'm sure that he was aware of the potential of certain people that he had put into certain positions. In one of his last discourses on the Ranch I heard him say that "the Ranch had been designed to fail". OK, let's put everything into a big pot, give it plenty of energy, let it cook for a while and see what happens. Ka-voom, and then on to the next caravanserai.

The city that we built and any other work we might have done was always of secondary importance, almost an accidental byproduct, to inner processes that were happening, to our personal growth. We were given an incredible freedom and space to act out whatever we needed to act out, and use that collectively, as a vehicle for our growth. The commune may not have succeeded, but it was an invaluable teaching for so many of us, however much we were able to appreciate it at the time it was available. That is what really counts. The commune was not an end that was to be achieved, "only" a means.

I have noticed that to this day the reputation of the Ranch is a rather negative one. The organization in Poona as well as many individual sannyasins have a strong tendency to see it as a dark spot in our past, and would prefer if it hadn't happened quite that way. In New Age circles it is not uncommon that the Ranch is referred to as "Osho's fascist work camp", or something to that effect. Whether those people have been there at all in the first place or not, I don't think they are able to see the Ranch as what it really was, as just a teaching, way beyond the confinements of "good" and "bad", and to me that makes it the work of a truly great master.

What remains with me today is a deep gratitude (if I may be permitted to use the g-word) towards Osho, towards everybody who had been there, and, yes, to the Oregonians, who possibly to this day still don't know what hit them.

***

PART IV:
NOW WHAT?

-38-

I arrived in Santa Cruz with 30 bucks in my pocket. I was 37 years old by then and had practically no experience of how to make a living out in the world, and even less so in California.

Santa Cruz was (and largely, still is) a pretty laid-back town of about 60,000 inhabitants, about an hour's drive down the coast from San Francisco, at the north end of Monterey Bay. Up to the sixties, Santa Cruz had been a sleepy little fishing town where many Italian immigrants had settled. That changed when the University of California opened a campus there, and subsequently it had become a mecca for all kinds of young folks. Just about any subculture you can think of has a strong following there. There are all kinds of activists ("Save the Whales!"), surfers ("What's up, dude? Catch a wave?"), an amazing number of musicians and bands, deadheads, gays, hippies, punks, skins, you name it. New Age-wise, it is a supermarket, California-land at its best. During the late seventies and early eighties, there had been a lot of sannyasins living there, and many of them were returning after the Ranch.

With that many freaks in town it made it in many ways easier to live there, I didn't stick out as much as I might have in other places. (And what made it even easier was that sometime during the last weeks on the Ranch, Osho had lifted the requirement that we were to wear only red clothes - now any color clothes were fine, and no *mala* any more, either.) What made it harder to survive in Santa Cruz was the fact that there were so many of us who wanted to live there. That drove the rents up, and kept the wages down, a perfect example of the law of supply and demand.

Nevertheless, existence provided. I always made the right connections and met the right people. Within days, I was working for a temporary agency. The lady who was scheduling the jobs there happened to like me and kept me busy. After a few weeks Devika and I had enough money together so that we could move into our own apartment. It turned out though that we were heading into different directions, and eventually split up. By that time, I was working in a carpentry shop, where I was making patio furniture and bookcases. That lasted for about half a year, and I moved on to a remodeling job with a couple of sannyasins. (One of those guys meanwhile got himself enlightened and now makes his living as a satsang wallah by the name of Arjuna. Then, he had done electrical work and had struck me as being pretty much of a regular guy. I guess you can never tell.)

By the spring of 1987 I seemed to have it made. I was working for a small mail order company, writing invoices and packing parcels. The stuff we were selling was quite interesting - it was free form crystalline amino acids, and our clientele consisted mainly of body builders and health freaks. After a lot of back and forth, I had myself a steady job.

Still, it hadn't all been a bed of roses. Many of us had left the Ranch with our heads in the clouds, full of great plans of how we were going to take the world out there in storm, how we were going to be just raking in the dough. There was a lot of disillusionment that happened and often a rather rough awakening to the harsh realities of the rat race.

As far as I went, I had in some instances been amazingly naive. Hell, I didn't even know how to fill out a job application. The ones I sent out while still doing temp-work I had completed very truthfully, in particular regarding my work background. There wasn't very much I could have put down anyway, so I just stated honestly what I had done and where, including "18 months of Rajneesh Security", on Osho's Ranch. In one instance I was invited for a job interview which, as far as I could tell, went rather well. My prospective employer, some carpenter looking for a helper, seemed to be a nice enough person, but told me after the interview was over that he had never had the intention to hire me - he'd just been curious what kind of a guy I was that had sent in an application like that.

So, pretty fast I learned that I had to reinvent myself, that I had to come up with a work- and personal history that was tailored to what they wanted to see, that was conclusive and that I'd be able to back up. As sad as it was, in order to survive I had to learn how to lie. My greatest asset, though, proved to be not any work skills I might have had, but my attitude towards the whole game, and for this my time with Osho had prepared me very well. Whatever happened was just the next thing that came along in life, no big deal, I did what I could do, as well as possible, and that was that.

To the east of Santa Cruz there is a coastal range covered by beautiful redwood forests, the Santa Cruz Mountains, and it was there that I was to have one of the great love affairs in my life. Oh, I just loved the redwoods. Early in the 20th century most of the virgin forests there had been cut down – it was mostly with that wood that San Francisco was rebuilt after the 1906 earthquake. The hills were bare for a while, but since the redwood tree is a conifer that has the ability to grow sprouts out of its own stumps, the forest quickly regrew, largely unaided by humans. If you take a walk there today, you can still see the fire-blackened stumps of the old trees, surrounded by younger trees that by now might be 70 or more years old themselves. Besides the sequoias, as they are also called, there are some hardwoods, namely oak and madrone.

Although it is a second-growth forest, it has a wildness and an aliveness and a beauty to it that totally fascinated me and that was so much unlike the forests I had come to know in Europe.

A sannyasin friend, Prembuddha, owned a parcel of 55 acres (22 hectares) of prime redwood forest way up in the mountains, where he lived with Magdalena, his lady friend, in a small cabin with a large woodstove that had been fashioned out of an old oil drum. When I went up there it seemed to me that I was entering a fairytale land, and soon it became a second home to me. I built myself a tent platform, atop a couple of old stumps, four feet above the ground and surrounded by a small grove of tall trees. It was overlooking a meadow with a huge, old redwood in the center that we called the Buddha Tree.

I went up there many a weekend, hanging out and helping with the chores. In particular, I enjoyed splitting wood, two foot long sections that were set upright and then split lengthways with the help of a long-handled and well worn-in maul. And there was just nothing like firing up that ol' stove when there was a rainstorm coming down in the winter, with a pot of Prembuddha's world - famous chili beans simmering on top of it, and with Leela the cat purring away in some corner.

***

-39-

As I mentioned, there was quite a New Age scene in town. After having been in Poona and on the Ranch for so long, I was a bit curious as to what was happening out here. There were all sorts of spiritual groups, from the Hare Krishna to a Subud temple and all kinds of Christian sects. In the mountains, there were a few Buddhist and Tibetan centers and monasteries. Readings? No problem. Astrology, palm, aura, past life, anything. Tarot readings were even advertised on TV. The town was overflowing with massage therapists, and featured a couple of massage schools. Channeling was a hot item in California, there were all kinds of disembodied entities around trying to give their message to humanity, so, naturally, there was a young woman in Santa Cruz who was channeling Shri Yukteshwar (the guru of Yogananda – the one with the autobiography).

Have you ever come across a walk-in? What that is, it's when an entity that does not have a body to live in somehow takes up residence in somebody else's body. (What happens to the soul of *that* body I could not find out, but that's not *my* problem.) In any case, in Santa Cruz I knew this guy who was dead sure that he, in fact, was such a walk-in, a body-snatcher. On the outside, he was the son of a Californian hippie-couple and a successful chiropractor, with a strong tendency to be an over-achiever. And he was totally at a loss as to what the fuck he was supposed to be doing on this planet.

By and large, I found the whole scene a bit naive. For my taste, there was too much saving-the-world stuff going on. To me, it's consciousness first, and everything else happens as a consequence. I can help others only to the extent that I have cleaned up my own act, so that's where my first priority is. Sure, the world appears to be in a very sorry state, but what do I really know about where it may be heading? Who am I to interfere? Now, that doesn't mean I won't help that old granny across the street, but I do that rather on a spontaneous basis, I don't have any big plan. To me, it seems that everybody out there is trying to mess around with everybody else's lives, blaming everybody else for anything, and nobody knows what is really going on - except for a few awakened beings among us, and the only thing they can do that is of any value is to help us wake up, to whatever might be beyond the veil of our dreams.

There was one group, though, that attracted my interest. Through a flyer I had learned about a "Society of Abidance in Truth" (SAT), where satsangs were held once a week. At that time I did not really know what a formal satsang was, in its true generic sense, except that when we had sat with Osho while he was in silence we'd called that satsang. So, on a Sunday night in early 1987, I went. The satsang was held in a small hall, with a capacity crowd of 50 or 60 people in attendance. The teacher who held the satsang went by the name of "Master Nome", or simply "The Sage", and he was seen as an awakened being, in the lineage of Ramana Maharshi. He could have been anywhere in his thirties or forties, had his hair closely cropped, and was wearing loose pajama pants and an Indian-style shirt, all in white. We sat in silence for maybe 20 minutes, and then he gave a short advaita-based talk (without notes) and moved on to answer questions from the audience. He spoke in a way that was crisp and clear, and he had a beautiful sense of humor (one of my favorite lines of his referred to academic titles as "decorated ignorance").

I quite enjoyed myself, but it was not until I had left and was walking home under a starry sky that I started to focus my awareness more towards my inside. Something in me clicked, and I realized, "Yes, that was just how it felt like to be in Osho's presence!" Something in me had recognized the taste of that energy field, had remembered. Now, that got me thoroughly intrigued. Here I was, far from Poona where Osho meanwhile was again, but going there was out of the question because at the time I didn't have the financial means. It was not that I was desperate to go back. I was fine where I was, but to have a place right in town where I could recharge my batteries, I certainly couldn't ignore that.

I went for several more satsangs, until I was approached by people from SAT who, in a nice way, made it clear that I should become a member of the group if I wanted to continue to come. This I did not want to do. I might have felt quite at home with the Sage, but not so much among the kind of people he had attracted in the group around him. However nice and friendly, they appeared a bit too straight and yuppie-ish to me, they came across as a bit phony and repressed. It's not that I questioned their validity as spiritual seekers, but they were certainly a different brand than Osho's sannyasins. And my commitment was really somewhere else. So, at least for the time being, I continued on my path without the Sage.

However, I had learned a lesson that was to be of great importance in later years. If I met someone that claimed to be awakened, or if people inferred that quality to somebody, I had a way to check that. If I could catch that vibe, then, at least for me and for my own purposes, that was the truth.

***

-40-

In the summer of 1987 I moved into a small cabin in the redwoods near the mountain community of Brookdale, from where I was commuting by bus to my job, and on the weekends I went visiting my friends further up in the mountains. I was living comfortably, had my fun and I did not seem to be lacking anything.

Actually, I was quite thrilled to be living in California. I had always had a soft spot for the States, and my present life seemed to be the fulfillment of a dream I'd had for a long time. Back in 1967, during the Summer of Love, I had started to sense that there was something very special about California, and then there was all that great music that was coming from there. Ah, San Francisco ... but obviously, that hadn't been the time for me to be there.

Now, many years later, I still felt that vibe somewhat alive, particularly in Santa Cruz. I also saw that California had more dimensions to it than just that. In many different ways, it appeared that it was the cutting edge of western civilization. Just go to a natural foods store (or to a supermarket) there, and you'll see what I mean. And the center of modern technology, Silicon Valley, was just "over the hill", on the other side of the Santa Cruz Mountains. A friend of mine who had grown up there in the sixties had told me that then it had been mostly fruit orchards there, and now it was a smoggy nightmare of industrial parks, office parks, high-rises, housing developments, shopping malls, and endless eight-lane freeways. I guess if you take the components that the "American dream" is made up of and bring them to their logical conclusion, that's what you get.

Generally, I felt that there I had more freedom to do what I wanted to do and to be how I wanted to be than anywhere else in the world. There were a multitude of different life styles available, and there were a zillion things "to do", to keep you occupied, to play around with. Everybody was "into" something or other. A major part of the economy was geared to provide the means, and there were noticeably less rules and regulations. Yes, it is still the land of unlimited possibilities, at least seen relatively. If you're the entrepreneurial type (which I am certainly not), with a couple of good ideas, a few years of hard work and a bit of luck you can still make a fortune. And you also run a greater risk than elsewhere to end up in the gutter. There was a stunning amount of people that populated the streets and parks of Santa Cruz that were just down on their luck, homeless, sick, neglected, uncared for.

What I found quite amazing was the contrast between that "freedom" and a prevailing puritanism that expressed itself in a very prudish attitude towards sex and over-regulative laws concerning alcohol, tobacco and drugs. And the nationalism they've got going there ... if the Germans would display only a fraction of that, there would be an international outcry. Well, I guess the Americans have their issues, too, that they need to work on a bit. I'm not saying anybody is better than anybody else - everybody is fucked up, only differently so.

Of course, I'm not excluding myself there. Over the past few years, I'd had quite a reluctance to come to terms with certain aspects of my national origin, which had even gotten to the point that I refused to speak German, and would do so only if it could not be avoided without creating an embarrassment. I didn't want to have anything to do with anything German, and, quite befittingly, had ended up living in a place just about as far away from the fatherland as possible. I found it quite easy to slip into a somewhat different personality by just speaking a different language. That way I could put some of my issues on a backburner, but I noticed that it also created a distance from which I could see some things a lot clearer.

So, "California dreamin'" kept me busy for a while, until at some point in late fall it started to feel that something was missing in my life. Osho and the commune were calling me inside. I tallied up my savings - hmm, not bad, and didn't waste any more time. I quit my job, moved out of my cabin and stashed my belongings on a rack that I had suspended underneath my tent platform. In early January 1988 I left, with a one-way ticket to India and 7,000 dollars in cash in my pocket.

***

-41-

It felt great to come back to Poona (and that it remains for me; sorry, I'm not one of those politically correct "Pune"-sayers). Sure, the city had changed, and I cannot say for the better. For one thing, the pollution had gotten really bad. There also seemed to be a lot more people, although in India, wherever you went, there were always masses of them, so who can really tell? And the city had grown beyond Koregaon Park. Where before there had been only fields (and the bamboo hut villages of sannyasins), there were now cheap apartment buildings, dozens of them. The Ashram itself, well, who really cares, as long it was still there. Hey, it felt good just to get into a rickshaw and say, "Ashram, baba!" Before I knew it, we came to a screeching halt in front of the still so familiar main gate, the "Gateless Gate". Strangely enough, everybody was dressed in any color clothes, no robes, and no *malas*. Somehow a whole new generation of sannyasins seemed to be here, the majority of them dressed neatly and well groomed. It looked like our hippie-days were finally over. And the number of Germans and Japanese here had increased significantly - the Ashram was literally crawling with them.

Still, I ran into so many old friends that it took me half the morning to just make it from the main gate to Krishna House, hugging and chatting away merrily.

Osho's body had not been well, and there had been phases when he didn't come out for discourse. I was lucky, though, and got my first treat within a few days. Ah, to sit with him again and be showered by that energy ... it seemed like the only thing I'd ever want in my life.

I took a couple of days to get myself organized, and then started to work, in the subscription department of the Rajneesh Times. Maybe a month or so later I was asked if I would like to become a guard at Lao Tzu House. Now, that was right where the Old Man was living, and it didn't take me a moment's hesitation to accept.

There was only a very limited number of people that had access to Lao Tzu, a few that lived there and a few more that worked there, mainly in the library. This was to give Osho a bit of space, and also for security reasons, so the guards at the wrought- iron gate had to have their act pretty well together. There was another guard position further down the driveway, between the car port and the swan pond, and a third one in the garden, next to Chuang Tzu Auditorium. The air here was thick with Osho's energy, you could almost cut it with a knife. During the day, there was a certain amount of activity around the house, so the attention was focused more outward, but the nights were exceptionally special.

I loved going on a "round" at night, which one of us would routinely do every hour or so. This took me to some inside parts of the house (the hallways were lined with glassed-in bookcases containing Osho's library), up onto the roofs, and then particularly through the garden that resembled more a tropical jungle. There were a few overgrown pathways leading through it, and my favorite part of the round was to just feel my way along those paths, without using the flashlight that I was carrying, almost becoming one with my surroundings. Needless to say that it was pitch-black in there, and, of course, I had to be as quiet as a mouse. There was a small lawn in front of Osho's window (that was off-limits to everyone at almost any time), and at the edge of that lawn there stood a large, ancient and very beautiful almond tree. Among the guards it was understood that if you went on a round during the night, it could include going up to the almond tree and spending a bit of time there. And, between you and me, there was nothing like sitting down under that tree for a while at two or three in the morning, it was just pure magic.

The day shifts in the garden were quite different due to a lot of building activity in and around Chuang Tzu Auditorium. Workers were tearing the guts out of that place and, by and by, rebuilding it into what was to be a new bedroom for Osho. It almost broke my heart to see the place demolished where I had spent such beautiful times during Hindi discourses and darshans back in the old Poona days. And when Osho's new room was finally ready for him to move in more than a year later, from what I heard he spent a couple of nights there and then moved back into his old bedroom.

It certainly felt different being in the commune these days. As Osho had put it, this was his "third and last commune". There was no big carrot hanging in front of our nose in form of the "new commune", to keep everybody excited and motivated, as in Poona I. Nor did it appear that several thousand of us were going to be here together, with a large, consistent core group, as on the Ranch.

There were still people here that had no plans to go anywhere else, as long as Osho was here, but their number was comparatively small. There were also still quite a few sannyasins working at the Ashram, probably a couple of hundred, but they were by far not enough for all the work that needed to be done, so a lot of Indian workers were hired, particularly to do menial jobs. There were still two or three thousand souls here at any given time, but most of them were returning after a few weeks, or at the most, months, to the lives and careers they had left behind in their home countries.

In many instances things were very much unlike the way they were going to evolve to in the later stages of Poona II. The buildings had not been painted black yet, nor had the pyramids been built. It was also before people were asked to wear red robes while in the Ashram, so I had no problem to continue wearing my beloved blue jeans there (which came in very handy when I was guarding during those chilly winter nights). Nor had the "White Robe Brotherhood" come into being, although the seed stages were already clearly discernible. Personally, I had never liked that hullabaloo with music, clapping and what not before and after discourse. I'd prefer the pin-drop silence that had been there in the old times, any time.

It was also Osho who had changed. When I had first come to Poona, Osho had been a man in his prime, full of fiery energy, while now he was coming across as a bit more granddaddy-like. He was giving discourses again, his health permitting, but to me the discourses seemed to be lacking quite a bit of the temperament they'd had in the seventies. He was also speaking a lot slower.

It was very apparent that his body was not well, and he looked increasingly frail. It had always been a treat just to watch him move his hands while he was speaking, incredibly beautiful and graceful mudras. Now it seemed that he could use his arms and hands, in particular the left one, only with great difficulty. On his way in and out of Buddha Hall he almost didn't seem to be touching the floor. While he had always been moving very lightly on his feet, we were now afraid that he might actually fall, that something as small as an errant breeze might topple him over.

One of his trademark moves throughout the years had been that, after sitting down, he'd slide the thong off his left foot, and then cross his left leg over his right knee. Always that way around, never otherwise, and he'd remain in that position for the whole duration of the discourse, or satsang. Then, sometime in the fall of 1988, he stopped doing that, from one day to the next, and continued sitting with his legs parallel to each other, both feet on the floor.

Still, he had his bag of tricks. He liked to tease Niskriya, the German cameraman who used to stand with his camera a short distance from the podium to videotape the discourses. He jokingly called him "stonehead", because at some point he had shaved his head, repeatedly made fun of his "Germanness", and eventually, at the end of a discourse, even goaded him into raising his right arm in the "Hitler greeting", the way Germans had greeted each other during the Third Reich. The audience was totally stunned as Osho in turn raised his own right arm the same way. So, there the two of them stood, facing each other with raised right arms, and you can bet that some of the Germans that were present were going through a lot of stuff.

The next evening, Osho defused the situation by raising both of his arms in greeting at the end of the discourse, and he added the exclamation, "yahoo!" to that, which was taken from a juicy joke that he had just told. And thus started the yahoo-phase of the commune, where sannyasins were seen greeting each other by raising both arms and exclaiming, "yahoo!"

During what were to be my final weeks in Poona, Osho delivered one of his last masterstrokes. He demolished his own name, Bhagwan Shree Rajneesh, the name that he was known by worldwide, and the name by which we as his disciples were referring to him, a name that was very dear to us, a very deep thing. First he tossed the "Bhagwan" ("The Blessed One") out the door. He briefly adopted the name "Maitreya" ("Friend" - Gautama Buddha had said he would come back to the world known as "Maitreya"), played around with that some, cracked a few jokes over it, only to drop that, too. Next came "Shree Rajneesh Zorba the Buddha", but a short time later he discarded all of that, including "Rajneesh" (meaning "Lord of the Night"), the name he had acquired as a kid due to his regal bearing. (His legal name has been Chandra Mohan Jain.)

Eventually, he came up with the name "Osho", but not until after I had gone. ("Osho" is derived from William James' word oceanic, meaning "dissolving into the ocean". It has also been used historically in the Far East, meaning, "the blessed one, on whom the sky showers flowers".) These days, I privately sometimes still call him Bhagwan, and I don't think he minds that, wherever he may be now (but don't tell anyone, please).

***

Discourse, ca. 1988

Osho's samadhi

California New Age cowboy, 1995: Now what?

-42-

The only thing I was really into during those times was my work. I had always had a strong tendency to be a loner, and now even more so. My social contacts were largely limited to occasional chats over a cup of coffee with old friends, but I took less and less interest in what else was going on in the commune. Everybody else was totally excited about the "Mystic Rose", a new therapeutic- meditative group Osho had just created, but not me. There was also a lot of Tibetan stuff going on that was getting quite popular - but pulsing? I couldn't care less. In a way, I slowly withdrew from the commune, yet, I still had my time in Osho's garden to keep me going.

After half a year in India I flew to Bangkok to get a new visa. We were doing everything by the book now, no more overstaying your visa for months or years altogether. And you had to be careful when entering India again. If the immigration officials at the airport found out that you were a sannyasin or were going to visit the Ashram, it was very likely that you were refused entry - I've known a few cases. They also had lists of sannyasins that were persona non grata, possibly dating back to the final days of Poona I. One of them beat the system by going on to Nepal, and then entering India on the land route. I managed fine, though, came right back from Bangkok and continued guarding at Lao Tzu.

During that time, it was coping with the Indian reality outside the Ashram that was getting at my nerves more and more, the whole dirt and stink and noise and, of course, the omnipresent babas that were hassling me. And I started to miss California. One night, I was sitting with one of the other guards, a relatively "young" sannyasin, at the gate, and I was getting a bit into a sharing mode, bitching about living in India and about a couple of things that were bugging me at the Ashram. He looked at me, and said, "I don't know what you mean, I totally love it here." That clicked something in me. Back in Poona I, I had felt exactly like him, nothing else had mattered at all, and it slowly began to sink in that my time here might be coming to a close. It was Osho and his garden that were the main factor still keeping me here.

Towards the end of 1988 I felt increasingly that Poona was not the place I wanted to be. This did not mean that to me Osho was any less enlightened. Rather, from the omnipotent, all-knowing master he had been to me during my earlier years as a sannyasin (and I had obviously needed that then) he had turned more into a very dear spiritual friend on the path. Somehow or other it became clear to me that it was time for me to bid farewell to him and the commune and continue on my own, "out in the world".

Probably the hottest privilege we got being Lao Tzu guards was that about every two weeks we'd get a front row seat at discourse. And not just any front row seat, but in the first row, and way over on the side, the last seat on either the left or the right side. This counted as a guarding position, and we had to keep our eyes open and be on the alert should anything happen that might endanger Osho. No spacing out there, swami. We took turns covering that position, during times that we were not on shift.

I had worked until the last day before I was to leave, and had managed to arrange that for my last discourse I could sit in the front row, as a kind of a farewell treat. I ended up taking the seat on Osho's right side. From there, I could also see behind the partition that was in front of the actual exit of the hall, a freestanding marble wall behind his chair. At the end of the discourse, Osho would give his namaste, and then walk over to his left, around the corner of the partition, and then, in a right-hand turn, exit the hall to get into the waiting Rolls-Royce that would take him back to Lao Tzu House. So, from that seat, I could see Osho after he'd gone behind that partition, just before leaving the hall. Normally, after being done with his namaste, he'd lower his hands and walk out, not doing anything in particular, just walking and minding his own business. On that evening, however, behind the partition, he looked up, briefly, and straight into my eyes. And there was no expression in that look; he was just totally, one hundred percent present, *there*.

By all appearances, I was entering a new phase as a sannyasin, from career sannyasin to free agent. I've never had the impression that I was "dropping" sannyas, or that anything I had learned or experienced was suddenly of no value any more, or had been wrong. On the contrary, every day I've spent with Osho and the commune has been a blessing, and I wouldn't want to miss even a single one. My years with him have been the defining time of my life, and I feel I've hit the jackpot with that one. (Sometimes I wonder whether I needed all those years with Osho because I've got such a thick head ...) Now my time had come where I had to continue without that supportive and protective environment, like a young bird that got kicked out of the nest by its parents. The nature of the teaching had changed; I had to be able to recognize it in whichever disguise it might appear on my path, on my own.

Sure, on some level I miss the commune an awful lot (particularly the ma-department!). To this day, I have dreams about Osho and sannyasins, sometimes even about distinct people I'd known then. Often I wonder where all my friends are today, and I hope they're all doing fine (ultimately, I know they are). The commune had consisted of an incredible collection of people, where it had been more than nourishing enough to just be amongst them. It's that aliveness, openness and rebelliousness, that willingness to look at oneself and deal with whatever comes up that I find conspicuously absent out here. It's an emotional desert, not much love and laughter. And by this I mean more the general climate than the exceptions that are there, too.

I have never been back to Poona. To some extent, I have been following what has been happening there, and from what has been coming across, how the way of being in Osho's energy field is manifesting itself nowadays, I have not felt that it is my place any more, in particular since his mahaparinirvana on January 19, 1990. On the outside, the "meditation resort" feels a bit too glitzy to me, and maybe that's only because I'm still a hippie at heart and have never made the transition to being a yuppie. As far as the inner substance is concerned, I don't know whether Osho's teachings are being watered down ("Osho Lite"), or whether they are getting adjusted to the needs of our present time. Maybe what is happening there is what is always happening to a Buddha's teaching once he is gone, if an organization consisting of unawakened people is taking care of the "inheritance". But much more importantly, the torch is being carried by each individual sannyasin in his or her being true to what Osho has imparted to them. That is his real legacy.

I have seen some interviews with members of the "Inner Circle" on video or in print and, to be honest, the general energy has totally put me off. What they are lacking in humbleness they are making up for with a beaming self-righteousness. Like good pundits, they always have a suitable Osho quote ready to support their argument, and, by all means, you can find an Osho quote to suit almost any purpose - but the quote is not worth much without the context it had originally been given in. What makes me most suspicious that there is a nigger there somewhere in the woodpile (as they used to say in the old West) is that being associated with Osho is becoming a respectable thing. Osho never gave a damn about respectability, he only kicked ass, whatever the consequences.

I was feeling rather incredulous when I heard that in 2001 there had been no celebration at the Ashram for Osho's birthday, which would have been his 70th. Now, what's wrong with that? After all, he had been here in his body to teach us, so why not celebrate the day of his birth? Is this what a "guruless ashram" or "religionless religion" is all about? Gimme a break!

Nonetheless, it is good that the place exists, as it is. From what I heard, it is still a beautiful environment to meditate in, and a lot of seekers are getting help on their path. And it is good that the old place is gone. No, I didn't burn that bridge, it is just not there anymore, and that makes it easier for me to go on ahead.

***

-43-

In January 1989 I left India for Germany, where I visited my parents whom I had not seen in many years, and then continued on to California. Since I had some savings left there was no need to go to work right away, so I decided to take some serious time off in the redwoods. On Prembuddha's land, I moved into a tiny guest cabin that I had helped build a couple of years before. It was precariously perched high up on a steep slope, and when I looked out of the large front window it felt like being up in a tree house. There was a propane gas heater for warmth and a kerosene lamp for light, and I didn't need much more than that. I was totally content just to sit there and look out the window at those beautiful trees, or to watch the rain when it was pouring down during a storm. I wasn't worried about a thing. When it got warmer in the spring, I moved into my tent, and for entertainment there was always some carpentry work to do or some wood to split, or, most importantly, a good cup of coffee to share with my fellow mountain folks. Yes, that certainly was the good life in the redwoods.

Eventually, I was starting to feel a bit itchy. I wanted to be closer to town, so in June I moved into a sannyasin house that was located in a picturesque semi-rural area south of Santa Cruz.

There were six of us, all Ranch veterans. Due to our connection with Osho and to our experiences on the Ranch and in Poona there is a strong heart connection among sannyasins, even though we may not have known each other then. I still feel this connection today, at chance meetings that happen from time to time, or towards old friends that are somewhere out there in the world and that I haven't seen in years. This bond made living in that house a very extraordinary experience. Sure, there were some tensions. One of the ladies had a big trip going with me (maybe because she was Jewish and I was German, who knows), but one thing we had learned around Osho was to deal with situations like that. Normally, the group energy in the house was very light, and we had a lot of fun with each other.

At some point I couldn't help noticing that every Sunday morning everybody would get together in our "family room", a converted garage - no, not to have a satsang, but to watch professional football on TV, first one game, and then another one. Before I knew it, I was watching, too, and it didn't take long to make me a big fan of the San Francisco 49ers. (During those years, the Niners had one of the best teams in pro football, and in that season ended up winning the Super Bowl, 55:10 against the Denver Broncos, with plenty of vintage Montana-to-Rice. Time for some serious celebration at our house!) As far as work was concerned, I did a few carpentry jobs, but I also was left with a lot of time for myself, to meditate, or to just take it easy.

***

-44-

For many years I have had the feeling that there is something very special about the time that we are living in. Far from being a doomsday freak, I still feel that there is certainly something in the bush (no pun intended regarding George W.). Osho has frequently made remarks about a possible quantum leap in the development of human consciousness, and that unless that happens, humanity is doomed. I have read about certain prophecies of the Mayans, of the Hopis and of others, all pointing to our present time, and what they agree on is that we're heading into pretty rough times, all kinds of disasters, upheavals and such. It's certainly not going to be very comfortable, and at some point we might not be getting our bowl of cornflakes anymore in the morning.

When I look at the state the world is in I can't help but seeing myself right in the middle of the Kali Yuga, a very dark time consciousnesswise. I have often wondered what it was that I've done to have been born into such an ignorant culture. I mean, let's face it, the level of ignorance out there is just stunning, and I have the feeling that it's going to get worse before it'll get any better.

Admittedly, it is not possible to say what is actually going to happen, how the Age of Aquarius is going to unfold. Nor can you outwit existence, so you'd better stay alert and be ready to meet anything that might come your way. It's not good to get caught with your pants down.

Some time before I had left for India the last time I had come across one of Nostradamus' predictions that spoke of a major earthquake that was going to happen in California in May 1988. At least, that was the interpretation. Now, I didn't plan my life around that, but was somehow glad that in 1988 I happened to be where I was, far from there and at the feet of my master. Come May, I was monitoring the news as closely as was possible for me there, and, lo and behold, nothing happened. Oh, well.

Then, back in Santa Cruz, I was visiting friends on a very nice and sunny day in the fall. We were just outside their house, on their driveway, about to get into their car. It was October 17, 1989, 5.04 pm. All of a sudden, the earth under my feet seemed to be coming alive. I felt like I was standing on a wavy sea, being moved up and down by the rolling movement of the earth. Everything else seemed to be suspended, I had no feelings or thoughts, except deep down inside some kind of a wordless recognition like, "WOW! This is really something BIG that's coming down!" All I did was just stand there, with my left hand on my belly, riding it out and watching in awe. The quake lasted 15 seconds, and it was measured 7.1 on the Richter scale. The epicenter was on a mountain called Loma Prieta in the Santa Cruz Mountains, just 10 miles as the crow flies from the house I was living in.

I made it home, somehow, walking and hitching rides, since most of the public busses were not running. Many of the people I saw on my way seemed to be somewhat disoriented or in shock. I was relieved to see my house still standing - they do have very strict building codes in California that prevented more extensive damage. I will never forget how I came around the corner of our driveway and saw my old friend Veet who was just picking up my bicycle that had fallen over. It felt so good to see him, and the others, who by and by made it home, too.

The damage to our house was comparatively minor. A few windows were broken, there were a lot of cracks in the walls, some doors did not close properly. There was a crack that was at places almost an inch wide that had opened up across our driveway, and another one across the concrete slab that the floor our family room consisted of. Our hot water heater that also fed our heating system had been thrown off its base. In the whole house, all the cupboards, shelves and closets were bare. Everything was on the floor, in big, untidy heaps. In the kitchen there was a huge pile of food and broken dishes, even our fridge had been emptied. There was no running water or electricity, and the phone was out. It was quite a mess.

If anything, this showed us how fragile that net can be that modern man has woven to support himself and that generally is taken for granted. We had not set aside any emergency supplies, or extra water. Somehow, we salvaged a few batteries that we put into an old transistor radio to be able to listen to the emergency radio station that was providing us with news from around the Bay Area. We also managed to round up a few candles and a bottle of tequila that had survived the quake.

So, after dark, we sat there by candlelight, got drunk and tried to assess our situation. It was certainly a bonus that we'd all learned to deal with our feelings and were able to share, so we didn't get into any head trips or freak-outs. One factor that kept us a bit on edge was that there were quite a few aftershocks, throughout the night, and continuing for a couple of days. Some of them were rather strong, and there was no way of telling whether another major one was just around the corner.

The next day, we sent out an expedition to a nearby shopping center, which we found open, but charging exuberant prices for certain goods like bottled water. The physical damage to our house was eventually repaired, not so much of a problem (in fact, our landlord hired me to do most of the repair work, and I made some good money).

But for a long time afterwards I was still a touch jumpy - I might be in some building and a big truck might be rolling by, and upon feeling the ever so slight shaking of the house, some faint voice in me would be whispering, "Hey, is that a quake, or just a truck?" And up to this day, wherever I live, I have a supply of water, candles, batteries and some durable food stashed away. Maybe I'll never need it, but who is to know. Ultimately, though, I know that any preparation is only good up to a certain point, and beyond that I can only let go and trust.

***

-45-

There were still quite a few sannyasins in the area. Some had rented houses together, some were living by themselves, and we also had an Osho Meditation Center, Gandarva. There were satsangs now and then with great pot-luck lunches, Osho videos, parties and get-togethers.

Most notably, on one fine Saturday night there was this party way up in Carmel Valley on a remote farm where some sannyasins were living. I got there a bit late, so the place was already in full swing. In the farmhouse, a whole bunch of people were hanging out, and one of them was giving a rap on the Tao of multi-level marketing and its benefits for human kind, which didn't interest me very much. Outside, a ways up the hill there was a meadow with a big campfire that attracted my attention, and here I found what was very obviously the center of activities. There were dozens of people around the fire, lying there in piles and heaps, moaning and groaning (and all still fully clothed!), and in some mysterious way they seemed to be having a jolly good time. I stood there for a bit, somewhat amused, scratching my beard, until I was approached by some compassionate soul who informed me that, "Hey, we're all doing 'E' here," and whether I'd like a ticket, too. No contest, really, and before long I got immersed in the ecstatic goings-on myself. The only person I pitied a bit was this guy I noticed at some point later on through the haze out of the corner of my eye. He was standing there, off to the side, in his baseball cap and with a can of Bud Light in his fist, by all appearances some local hick who had spotted the fire on his Saturday nite cruise in his pick-up and had stopped to investigate. This dude clearly looked like he'd landed on some different planet.

However, by and by, the sannyasin scene lost its cohesion and started to disintegrate. Some people left town for greener pastures, some people left Osho, and everybody more or less went off into his own direction, doing his own thing. This certainly had an effect upon how I was evaluating the quality of life in Santa Cruz.

What had also happened was that the earthquake had hit our downtown area very hard, many of the brick buildings there had been damaged so badly that they had to be torn down. Before, there had been the "Pacific Garden Mall", a beautiful pedestrian area with many trees, a very nice place just to go to and hang out and listen to the street musicians. Now most of those trees were cut down, the whole area was cordoned off, a huge demolition- and construction site, and the local businesses were struggling to survive in tents that had been erected nearby.

And, finally, job-wise nothing had come together that had even the faint resemblance to something more long-term. Sure, my carpentry jobs earned me more than enough to pay my bills, but the whole thing was feeling rather impermanent. So, however nice my personal living situation was, I was starting to wonder if there was a life beyond Santa Cruz, although I didn't have a very concrete idea. I was up for grabs, so to speak.

It was at the 1989 New Year's Eve party at our local Osho center that I met Amba, a beautiful German lady. She had moved to Santa

Cruz a few months earlier, after having spent a year as a work-scholar at Esalen. Before long, we had a pretty intense relationship going, and the only clouds on the horizon were that she was planning to leave town in spring to go live on Formentera, a Spanish island in the Mediterranean. To cut a long story short, she left in April, and I followed in June. Once again, it was good- bye, California.

***

-46-

Formentera Fall

Stonewalls
And windtorn trees,
White house in the sun.
Quickly,
The lizard moves.

Yes, we had us some quality times, Amba and me and our passel of cats. There were gorgeous springs that gave way to hot summers, and cold and stormy and rainy winter days by the fireside, in our wonderful *finca* way out on the *campos*, on the Cap de Barbaria.

But there was no escaping from that one basic ingredient in life, from change. Eventually the situation played itself out, and, yet another time, I packed my bags and moved on ...

***

-47-

... to return to Santa Cruz in the spring of 1994. Although the novelty had worn off a bit, I quite enjoyed my life as a California New Age Cowboy. I rode my bike along scenic West Cliff Drive, went to great rock concerts at the Catalyst, soaked my bones in steaming hot tubs, and just loooved Mexican food ... can't beat those burritos! There were still some old sannyasin friends in town, and we'd get together on occasion to let the good times roll.

To support myself I worked a number of jobs, and they always happened to come along when needed. Typically, in the beginning they felt like a place in heaven, and later, towards the end, like a place in hell. Some of them I quit, at other times I was "let go". In one case I was very badly mobbed out of a job as an accountant at the Public Works Department of the County of Santa Cruz ... which in the long run probably was for the better - me as a public servant? Forget it.

However, by the time the summer of 1999 came around, I was getting some very clear messages from existence that I needed a radical change in the direction my life was heading. I contemplated on some of the sannyasin hot spots, Sedona, Santa Fe, Boulder ...

but what would I be doing there? Same old thing. It appeared that I had literally run out of places to go. Been there, done that, got the T-shirt.

So I decided to return to my roots, to that small town in Germany where I'd once set out from. And ultimately, does the place really matter? Wherever you go, there you are. I can't escape from where I'm at with myself. What does matter is that I recognize and accept the lessons that come along, that life so mysteriously and effectively places right in front of my nose.

At the time, the "why" wasn't so clear to me, but in hindsight it turned out do be a smart move. I did have some unfinished business there, with my parents, and with the place itself. I want to spare you the details, but honestly, I did my best, and applied whatever awareness I was able to come up with to the situation as it evolved. I do feel good about the whole thing, and time will tell whether it is good enough.

***

-48-

Even an incomplete tale like this should not be complete without somewhat of an account of where I'm at on my path. Yes, Osho's still The Man, and there is nothing much I can do about that, that is just the case. Still, it has felt fine to spend some time with a few other enlightened ones over the years, when they happened along. Sort of like in that old Stephen Stills song, "If you can't be with the one you love, love the one you're with".

When I returned to live in Germany in September 1999, I was totally out of touch with what was happening there New Age- wise. After all, I had been gone for 22 years, except for a few relatively brief visits. Somehow, I did not feel to continue on my path more or less on my own as I had in recent years. Following the message, "Find an awakened friend to sit with" that had gotten to me mysteriously, I started to look around. I was quite amazed to find that, besides all kinds of other things reminiscent of the scene in California, there were literally dozens of awakened people around that were doing their thing. Most of them were giving satsangs, some were more stationary, others were moving around quite a bit. Some of them were offering retreats, in Germany as well as abroad. To me, this was clearly the hottest thing going on in the scene, for those that were ready for it.

It wasn't much of a problem to obtain information about those "satsang teachers", as they were called. From what I read in New Age magazines in the form of CVs, interviews with them or articles by them, and from what I saw in their eyes in the photographs of them, some of them definitely seemed to be genuine, seemed to "have it", while others didn't attract me very much, to say the least. Unfortunately, there was not much happening in my vicinity. Most of them were based in big cities like Berlin or Hamburg, and particularly southern Germany seemed to be crawling with them. Bavaria, of all places, appeared to have become the German equivalent of California (while politically, it still is very much like Texas).

There was one of them that I liked especially, a guy named Samarpan. He was a sannyasin (we might even have run into each other on the Ranch since we had been there at the same time, but I didn't remember him) and had been awakened in a satsang with Gangaji. What he wrote in a magazine article about Osho rang so true and moved me so much, that I decided to give it a shot and sign up for one of the retreats he was offering. Sometime in the spring of 2000, I left a message on the answering machine of the people that were organizing the retreat, also sannyasins as I could tell by their names, and waited, and waited, and nothing happened. Eventually I called that number again and learned from a recorded message that the retreat was booked up. Well, sad as I was, I had to concede that that one hadn't been for me.

A bit earlier that year, I had come across a brief magazine article about another satsang teacher named Pyar ("Introducing: Pyar"). Also a sannyasin, she was based in Munich and had worked with Samarpan before and during her awakening. When I saw the picture of her that came with the article, there was something in me that commented faintly, but discernibly, "Oh, *her*", although I could not remember ever having seen her before, and in my mind's eye I could see her as a wise woman, walking through the woods and collecting herbs. I was totally surprised when later that spring I received a flyer from her in the mail which informed me about two retreats she was giving, in June and in September of that year. I was very much at a loss as to how I'd gotten onto that mailing list, but there was an immediate "yes" in me, and I went ahead and booked the first of the two retreats.

I arrived a bit early at the retreat, which was taking place in the small town of Gmund at the Tegernsee, a beautiful lake right at the northern edge of the Bavarian Alps. Pyar and her staff were still getting the place ready, and they asked me to just hang out a bit outside on the patio. I went outside, sat down, took a couple of deep breaths, and, hey, there it was again, that so familiar energy, which was the reason for which I'd really come. So right there and then, even before the first satsang, I decided that I'd be attending the retreat in September as well, and then some more.

After a while Pyar came out to say hello, and she was somewhat curious as to how I'd gotten there, because she had never seen me in any of her satsangs. It took us a bit of figuring until we were able to put two and two together - what had happened was that the people I had called regarding the Samarpan retreat were also working with Pyar at times, and they had passed my address on to her staff. Another mystery unveiled!

Now, in the late summer of oh-two and with my seventh retreat coming up, all I can really say is that I feel very much at home with her and with the sangha that is starting to crystallize around her. The retreats are all "silent retreats", except during the satsangs, when we have the opportunity to ask questions. I'd say that about a third of the participants are sannyasins. There are quite a few people that I've met on three or four different retreats, and I've made some very good friends. Sure, there is a bit of chit-chat going on, even on a silent retreat, but it is becoming apparent to me that being together in silence can be much more of a factor in getting closer to each other than a lot of talking; you connect somewhere deeper than just on the mind level.

But the main reason I've kept coming is that I feel that Pyar is creating the perfect space for me to work on myself, or however you want to call it. It's not that I have very many questions on a verbal level. Actually, I wouldn't mind if there was more time to just sit in silence during the satsangs, but that doesn't matter very much. The way I see it, the *real* work is happening on a subtle energy level. Generally, I do feel totally accepted there for what I am and where I'm at and what I need to do, and that nothing is being imposed upon me. And, which is important for me, Osho is very much present there.

In my everyday life out in the world, I have been more and more focusing on just meeting each moment as it comes, and on allowing what wants to happen anyway. There is nowhere to go and nothing to achieve - the path itself is the goal. Sometimes input is needed from me, but that comes more out of the situation as it evolves. And the more I approach life like that, without the usual expectations, fears and other hang-ups, the more I've been getting into a harmonious flow, the more I've been flowing with the whole scene, and everything works out just fine. This same attitude I've tried to bring into the retreats. On a conscious level, I don't really know what's going on, and I don't care, either, as long as it feels right - and that it does.

The only relevant question in life is, "Who am I?", and the only thing I can ultimately do to find out about that is to let go, or rather, to allow a let-go to happen, and then I'll just see whatever is the case. As simple as that may sound, it is one extremely subtle business, so until then, I just sit patiently on my small meditation bench and try to be as alert as possible, sometimes focused more outward, sometimes more inward. But at the latest when I come out of a retreat and I'm having fun with just about anything that I do, and when I notice that my meditations are noticeably increasing in depth, and that this doesn't fade out after a few days but is getting better and better over time, then I know I must be on the right track.

As a person, Pyar never ceases to amaze me. One of her most striking qualities is her utter simplicity and unpretentiousness. After the satsangs, she hangs out with everybody else outside to have a smoke (Bavarian as she may be, she smokes "American Spirits" - this baby's come a long way!), and she is always open if somebody wants to talk to her about something, outside of the satsangs. During the meals, you might find yourself sitting at the same table with her, and, as a special treat, you might end up just looking into her eyes for a bit. (That one always really gets to me!)

Apart from that, she is exceptionally bright. In her "other" life, she is an MD, specialized in homeopathy and acupuncture, and she is still practising, full time. According to her autobiography "Reise ins Nichts" ("Journey into Nothingness", which has been a pretty hot item on the New Age scene in Germany), she had been one of those students who'd been getting mainly straight "A"s, without ever having to do a lot of homework for it. For many years she has been married to Nirdoshi, her high school sweetheart, a beautiful big bear of a guy, very much in contrast to her own rather slender self. He does her PR, plays *bhajans* together with a group of musicians before and after satsang, and gives great bear hugs. Also, there is nothing that she loves more than a juicy joke and a good glass of wine.

Spiritually, her strongest influences are Osho and Tibetan Buddhism, but she is just as much at home on other paths, such as Zen or Sufism. Yet, I don't see her as being confined by anything. She has her own very particular way of doing what she is doing, and that with a lot of wit and clarity and love. In satsang, I have seen her dealing with somebody's drama with the same ease as she showed when there was a seeker who was going through some extremely deep inner spaces and needed (and got) some expert guidance. On another occasion, there was someone who was obviously suffering from the "advaita disease" and who tried to drag her into a discussion in an attempt to prove some rather stupid point, while getting rather aggressive at the same time. Pyar did not waver even a fraction of an inch.

In personal encounters with her, like during short chats after satsang outside on the "Bankerl" (for the uninitiated - that's what they call a bench in Bavaria), most of the time I get a quite direct experience of where I'm *really* at, how much I'm still rooted in my mind, how fast my mind clicks in when it actually doesn't need to. I don't know if I've ever *really* met her, if I am capable to be with her on her terms, in silence. She is just too direct, too much just *there*, for me to be able to grasp it the way I function, to be able to truly respond to her. Usually, I have the feeling of lagging a step or two behind, and before I realize it, it's too late. Still, what comes across from her is nothing but understanding and love, so that at least I don't feel like a complete, muddleheaded fool. Every time it is a beautiful, small lesson, and I wonder how many more I still need to eventually "get it". And fuck knows what that may turn out to be.

***

-49-

And so I've been sitting here in this one-horse town, spinning this yarn - actually, most of it is quite true, to my best recollection. But however much I've been trying to focus on the moment, I have to admit that there are times when I wonder a bit about where I'm heading. Not that I'm fed up here or that I've got the highway blues or anything like that, I'm just a little curious.

Looking at my past, I've become somewhat careful with making any predictions, and there's really no way of telling what's around the corner, in those waning days of the Kali Yuga. As my journey on the pathless path continues, I can't help noticing that I am being coached, guided along by something that is much, much bigger than my small self, and my experience and insights are of an immense help to be able to cope with whatever situation comes along. That allows me to relax, with anything that might happen. As the saying goes and as we all know, "It ain't over till the fat lady sings!" If worse comes to worst, if all else fails, I can still go and sit under a pine tree and meditate and have a good time ... while freezing my ass off in the cold of the Harz Mountains winter. Unless ... maybe I'll end up underneath a palm tree - now, wouldn't that be something! Let's wait and see!

First winter rain - I plod on,
Traveller, my name.
- Basho

***

APPENDICES

APPENDIX "A":

SONG OF MEDITATION

All beings are from the very beginning Buddhas.
It is like water and ice:
Apart from water, no ice,
Outside living beings, no Buddhas.
Not knowing it is near, they seek it afar.
What a pity!
It is like one in the water who cries out for thirst;
It is like the child of a rich house
Who has strayed away among the poor.
The cause of our circling through the six worlds
Is that we are on the dark paths of ignorance.
Dark path upon dark path treading,
When shall we escape from birth-and-death?
The Zen meditation of the Mahayana
Is beyond all our praise.
Giving and morality and the other perfections,
Taking of the Name, repentance, discipline,
And the many other right actions,
All come back to the practice of meditation.
By the merit of a single sitting
He destroys innumerable accumulated sins.
How can there be wrong paths for him?
The Pure Land paradise is not far.
When in reverence this truth is heard even once,
He who praises it and gladly embraces it
Has merit without end.
How much more he who turns within

And confirms directly his own nature,
That his own nature is no-nature –
Such has transcended vain words.
The gate opens, and cause and effect are one;
Straight runs the way – not two, not three.
Taking as form the form of no-form,
Going or returning, he is ever at home.
Singing and dancing, all is the voice of truth.
Wide is the heaven of boundless Samadhi,
Radiant the full moon of the fourfold wisdom.
What remains to be sought?
Nirvana is clear before him,
This very place the Lotus paradise,
This very body the Buddha.

Hakuin
(1685 – 1768)

APPENDIX "B":

DESIDERATA

GO PLACIDLY amid the noise and the haste
And remember what peace there may be in silence.

As far as possible without surrender
Be on good terms with all persons.
Speak your truth quietly and clearly,
And listen to others, even the dull and ignorant;
They too have their story.
Avoid loud and aggressive persons,
They are vexatious to the spirit.
If you compare yourself to others you may become vain and bitter,
For always there will be greater and lesser persons than yourself.

Enjoy your achievements as well as your plans.
Keep interested in your career however humble;
It is a real possession in the changing fortunes of time.
Exercise caution in your business affairs,
For the world is full of trickery.
But let this not blind you to what virtue there is;
Many persons strive for high ideals,
And everywhere life is full of heroism.
Be yourself,
Especially do not feign affection.
Neither be cynical about love;
For in the face of all aridity and disenchantment
It is as perennial as the grass.
Take kindly the counsel of the years
Gracefully surrendering the things of youth.

Nurture the strength of spirit
To shield you in sudden misfortunes.
But do not distress yourself with imaginings.
Many fears are born of fatigue and loneliness.
Beyond a wholesome discipline,
Be gentle with yourself.
You are a child of the universe,
No less than the trees and the stars:
You have a right to be here.
And whether or not it is clear to you,
No doubt the universe is unfolding as it should.

Therefore be at peace with God,
Whatever you conceive Him to be;
And whatever your labours and aspirations,
In the noisy confusion of life,
Keep peace with your soul.
With all its shams, drudgery and broken dreams,
It is still a beautiful world.
Be cheerful.
Strive to be happy.

Max Ehrmann
(1872 - 1945)

(One of my all-time favorites ...)

APPENDIX "F":

THE FAMOUS "FUCK DISCOURSE"

"Beloved Bhagwan, I feel shocked when you use the word 'fuck'. What to do?"

"Sargamo, it is one of the most beautiful words. The English language should be proud of it. I don't think any other language has such a beautiful word. One Tom from California has done some great research on it. I think he must be the famous Tom of Tom, Dick and Harry fame. He says:

One of the most interesting words in the English language today is the word 'fuck'. It is one magical word: just by its sound it can describe pain, pleasure, hate, and love. In language it falls into many grammatical categories. It can be used as a verb, both transitive (John fucked Mary) and intransitive (Mary was fucked by John), and as a noun (Mary is a fine fuck). It can be used as an adjective (Mary is fucking beautiful). As you can see, there are not many words with the versatility of 'fuck'.

Besides the sexual meaning, there are also the following uses:
Fraud: I got fucked at the used car lot.
Ignorance: Fucked if I know.
Trouble: I guess I am fucked now!
Aggression: Fuck you!
Displeasure: What the fuck is going on here?
Difficulty: I can't understand this fucking job.
Incompetence: He is a fuck-off.
Suspicion: What the fuck are you doing?
Enjoyment: I had a fucking good time.
Request: Get the fuck out of here!
Hostility: I am going to knock your fucking head off!
Greeting: How the fuck are you?

Apathy: Who gives a fuck?

Innovation: Get a bigger fucking hammer.

Surprise: Fuck! You scared the shit out of me!

Anxiety: Today is really fucked.

And it is very healthy, too. If every morning you do it as a Transcendental Meditation - just when you get up, the first thing, repeat the mantra 'Fuck you!' five times - it clears the throat. That's how I keep my throat clear!

Enough for today."

Osho, The Book of the Books, Vol. XI,
Discourse 4, April 14, 1980

ACKNOWLEDGEMENTS

Special thanks go to Bhagawati, aka "the hub". It was her gentle persuasion, dedicated networking and skilful "editing with a feather" that made it possible to get this story published. More thanks go to Punya at Osho News, and to Atul and Naina at Osho World, for their respective vital contributions. It's been a delight working with all of you.

And foremost, there is Osho - this is all for him, about him, and through him. There are no words fit to express this, only tears of gratitude ...